HYMNS AND SACRED POEMS OF AUGUSTUS TOPLADY

As from the Lute soft Music flows,
Obedient to the skilful hand;
So, tun'd by Thee, *my spirit owes*
Her harmony to Thy command.

Touch'd by the finger of Thy love,
Sweet melody of praise I bring;
Join the enraptur'd hosts above,
And feel the bliss that makes them sing.

—Augustus Toplady

En, sanctos Manibus puris ut sumeret Ignes,
Vestalem se Musa facit; bene libera Curis,
Libera Deliciisque, Jocisque & Amore profano.

—Abraham Cowley

HYMNS AND SACRED POEMS

On a variety of divine subjects, comprising the whole of his poetical remains with a sketch of his life and poetry

Comprised of two books:
I. Poems on sacred subjects, wherein the fundamental doctrines of Christianity, with many other interesting points, are occasionally introduced. (1759)

II. Occasional hymns and poems, composed between the years 1760–1778, now for the first time collected and printed, without alteration or abridgment, from the originals, being the whole of the remaining poetical pieces. (1860)

By the Rev.

AUGUSTUS M. TOPLADY

Late Vicar of Broad Hembury, Devon

Published by Curiosmith.
Minneapolis, Minnesota.
Internet: curiosmith.com.

Previously published by Daniel Sedgwick, 1860.

The "Biographical Sketch" is from the 1860 Daniel Sedgwick edition of Toplady hymns.

The "Preface" is from the 1759 edition of Toplady hymns.

The "Contents" was added to this edition by the publisher.

ISBN 9781946145352

CONTENTS

CONTENTS *(Continued)*

BIOGRAPHICAL SKETCH OF THE REV. AUGUSTUS M. TOPLADY

The Rev. Augustus Montague Toplady, B.A., was the son of Richard Toplady, a major, who died at the siege of Carthagena soon after the birth of his son. His mother's maiden name was Catharine Bate. She was sister to the Rev. Julia Bate, and the Rev. Mr. Bate, rector of St. Paul's, Deptford; by whom they were married at the above church, December 21, 1737. They had issue—one son named Francis, who died in his infancy, and our author, who was born at Farnham, in Surrey, November 4, 1740. His godfathers were Augustus Middleton and Adolphus Montague, Esquires; in honor to whom he bore the Christian name of the one, and the surname of the other. He received the first rudiments of his education at Westminster School, where he early evinced a peculiar genius. While a student at that place he accompanied his honored parent in a journey to Ireland, to pursue claims to an estate which she had in that kingdom. Notwithstanding the solitary state in which his mother was left, she anxiously watched over him with the deepest sympathy of affection, and persevered in a plan for his education and future prospects, which were the principal concerns of her maternal solicitude. The son returned her tender care with the utmost affection. Indeed, so great was the obligation which he always conceived he owed her, that he never mentioned her but in words expressive of sensibility and gratitude.

As this son of the prophets was improving those natural talents he was so eminently endowed with, it pleased God in his providence, when he was about the age of sixteen, to direct his steps into a barn, at a place called Codymain, in Ireland, where a layman was preaching. The Word of God was fixed upon his conscience, "in demonstration of the Spirit and with power." Let it not rashly be deemed the enthusiasm of a visionist, or the *ignis fatuus* of religious distraction, when we assert, "That his faith did not stand in the wisdom of men, but in the power of God." There was nothing peculiar in the place, nor instrument, to work upon his fancy or passions; therefore, to attempt to explain the effect by any logical or metaphysical investigation would be ridiculous, while we have the Scriptures in congeniality with facts to inform us that, "it pleaseth God, by the foolishness of preaching, to save them that believe."

A few years after this memorable circumstance, Mr. Toplady reflects upon it in the following words—"February 29, 1768. At night, after my return from Exeter, my desires were strongly drawn out, and drawn up to God. I could, indeed, say that I groaned with the groans of love, joy, and peace; but so it was, even with comfortable groans that cannot be uttered. That sweet text, Ephesians 2:13, 'Ye, who sometimes were far off, are made nigh by the blood of Christ,' was particularly delightful and refreshing to my soul; and the more so, as it reminded me of the days and months that are past, even the day of my sensible espousals to the Bridegroom of the elect. It was from this passage that Mr. Morris preached on the memorable evening of my effectual call. By the grace of God, under the ministry of that dear messenger, and under that sermon, I was, I trust, brought nigh by the blood of Christ, in August, 1756. Strange that I, who had so long sat under the means of grace in England, should be brought near to God in an obscure part of Ireland, amidst a handful of God's people met together in a barn, and under the ministry of one who could hardly spell his name. Surely it was the

Lord's doing, and is marvellous! The excellency of such power must be of God, and cannot be of man; the regenerating Spirit breathes not only on whom, but likewise when, where, and as He listeth."

Further reference is made to his conversion in the last exhortation he gave, on Sunday, June 14, 1778, a few weeks before his death—"I was awakened in the month of August, 1755, but not, as has been falsely reported, under Mr. John Wesley, or any preacher connected with him. Though awakened in 1755, I was not led into a full and clear view of the doctrines of grace till the year 1758, when, through the great goodness of God, my Arminian prejudices received an effectual shock, in reading Dr. Manton's sermons on the 17TH of St. John. I shall remember the years 1755 and 1758 with gratitude and joy, in the heaven of heavens, to all eternity."

Our author early made it appear that he was not afraid of literary labor; the valuable years of his youth were devoted to useful and honorable studies rather than to frivolous occupations, such as too often engross the minds of young men at his age. He laid a solid basis for future years, and the superstructure was beautiful. Between the age of fifteen and eighteen, by way of relaxation from his studies, he employed himself in writing little poetic pieces, which were printed in a 12mo. volume at Dublin, in the year 1759. They are by no means deficient in spirit and force; some of the verses are truly poetical, and many of the thoughts new. Amidst the small inaccuracies of these juvenile compositions, there are indubitable marks of genius. The ardor of piety and religion, which brightened the morning of his life, was increased with luster in his maturer years.

Richly endued with a variety of gifts, and divinely instructed in those doctrines requisite for a Christian and a Minister, he received imposition of hands on Trinity Sunday, the 6TH of June, 1762. He entered upon the ministerial function not only as a scholar, and as one professing religion, but as an honest man. He mentions that he subscribed to the articles, homilies, and liturgy, five separate times, from principle; he did not believe them because he subscribed them, but subscribed them because he believed them. He was well persuaded that, after such an awful declaration made by every candidate for holy orders, the man that can draw back or palliate, for any sinister purpose, the doctrines he has subscribed, so as to insinuate himself into the favor of men, to avoid persecution, or for any aggrandizement, must be devoid of every upright principle, and openly prove himself an apostate from the Church, a traitor to the cause he once avowed, and a liar to the Holy Ghost. Shortly after his initiation into the ministry, he was inducted into the living of Blagdon in Somersetshire, which he soon resigned. In the year 1768 he took possession of the vicarage of Broad Hembury, in Devonshire, which he held until his death. The produce of the living did not amount to £80 *per annum*. He was by no means anxious for temporal profits, or desirous of pursuing ecclesiastical preferments. It was his chief aim to merit the highest, and to be content with the lowest. In this situation he composed the greater part of those writings which will be esteemed and valued while the genuine principles of Christianity continue to be revered.

It was the misfortune of our much loved friend to have a capacious soaring mind enclosed in a very weak and languid body; yet, this by no means retarded his intense application to study, which was often prolonged until two or three o'clock in the morning. This, and the cold moist air that generally prevails in Devonshire, which is extremely pernicious to weak lungs, it is more than probable, laid the foundation of a consumption, which terminated in his death. He endeavored to exchange his living for one in a southern part of the island, but failed in the attempt. As his strength and health were greatly impaired, he was advised by the faculty to remove to London, which he accordingly did in the year 1775, and notwithstanding his debilitated frame, he continued to preach a number of sermons in the churches, for the benefit of public charitable institutions.

Having no settled place in the metropolis to preach in, and many of his friends being desirous of receiving the advantages of his ministry, they procured, by an engagement with the trustees of the French Calvinist Reformed Church in Orange-street, Leicester-fields, their chapel for divine service, on Sunday and Wednesday evenings. Mr. Toplady accordingly delivered his first lecture there on Sunday, April 11, 1776, from Isaiah 44:22. It was on this spot that he closed his ministerial labors, a term of two years and three months. In his addresses from the pulpit in that chapel, he appeared often, as it were, divested of the body, and to be in the participation of the happiness that appertains to the church triumphant.

During the time of his ministry at Orange-street chapel, he published, in the year 1776, a collection of Psalms and Hymns, for public and private worship. The compositions are four hundred and nineteen in number: they are judiciously selected, and some of them altered where the phraseology appeared to him exceptionable. The whole tenor of them is truly evangelical. In an excellent and sensible preface, prefixed to this manual of sacred poetry, Mr. Toplady observes, "with regard to the collection, he could only say, that (excepting the very few hymns of his own, which he was prevailed upon to insert), it ought to be the best that has appeared, considering the great number of volumes (no fewer than between forty and fifty) which had, more or less, contributed to the compilation." Two spurious editions of this collection have been printed, but so much altered as to leave scarcely any resemblance to the valuable original, which abounds with the richest odors of gospel truth.

The apprehensions entertained for some time past, by those who loved him, that his health was on the decline, began now to be confirmed. For, on Easter Sunday, the 19TH of April, 1778, as he attempted to preach from Isaiah 26:19, "Thy dead men shall live, together with my dead body shall they arise," etc., his hoarseness was so great that he was obliged, after naming the text, to descend from the pulpit. But so ardently abounding was he in the ministry of the word, that when the least abatement in his disorder gave him a little strength, he entered upon his delightful work with that alacrity of spirit, as if he were in a state of convalescence. After this Sunday he preached four times, and on each occasion his words were to the congregation as if he should never see them more, until he met them in the kingdom of heaven.

We have followed this ambassador of Christ in his public career, and have now to behold him in the closing scene of his life. The doctrines of the gospel, which he so sweetly preached, and which were his constant theme in the house of his pilgrimage, proved his support and comfort, when his fabric was gradually falling to dissolution. His divine Master was pleased to confer peculiar honor upon him in his last hours, by sustaining him in that trying conflict, and by giving him a view of the glory that awaited him. The Psalmist's words were verified in him, that "light is sown for the righteous, and gladness for the upright in heart." How does the luster of what men call great vanish, and prove to be but an illusive shadow, when we view a believer in his dying moments, happy in the bright and unclouded prospect of eternal felicity!

We here introduce some of his observations and remarks committed to writing by those present. In conversation with a gentleman of the faculty, not long before his death, he frequently disclaimed with abhorrence, the least dependence on his own righteousness, as any cause of his justification before God, and said, that he rejoiced only in the free, complete, and everlasting salvation of God's elect by Jesus Christ, through the sanctification of the Holy Spirit. We cannot satisfy the reader more than by giving this friend's own relation of intercourse and conversation. "A remarkable jealousy was apparent in his whole conduct, for fear of receiving any part of that honor which is due to Christ alone. He desired to be nothing and that Jesus might be all, and in all.—His feelings were so very tender upon this subject, that I once undesignedly put him almost in an agony, by remarking the great loss which the Church of Christ would sustain by his death at this particular juncture.—The utmost distress was immediately visible in his countenance, and he exclaimed to this purpose, 'What, by my death? No! By my death? No.—Jesus Christ is able, and will, by proper instruments, defend his own truths.—And with regard to what little I have been enabled to do in this way, not to me, not to me, but to his own name, and to that only, be the glory.'

"Conversing upon the subject of election, he said, that 'God's everlasting love to his chosen people; his eternal, particular, most free, and immutable choice of them in Christ Jesus, was without the least respect to any work, or works of righteousness, wrought, or to be wrought, or that ever should be wrought, in them or by them: for God's election did not depend upon our sanctification, but our sanctification depended upon God's election and appointment of us to everlasting life.'—At another time he was so affected with a sense of God's everlasting love to his soul, that he could not refrain from bursting into tears.

"The more his bodily strength was impaired, the more vigorous, lively, and rejoicing, his mind seemed to be. From the whole tenor of his conversation during our interviews, he appeared not merely placid and serene, but he evidently possessed the fullest assurance of the most triumphant faith. He repeatedly told me, that he had not had the least shadow of a doubt, respecting his eternal salvation, for near two years past. It is no wonder, therefore, that he so earnestly longed to be dissolved and to be with Christ. His soul seemed to be constantly panting heavenward; and his desires increased the nearer his dissolution approached. A short time before his death, at his request, I felt his pulse; and he desired to know what I thought of it. I told him, that his heart and arteries evidently beat (almost every day) weaker and weaker. He replied immediately, with the sweetest smile upon his countenance, 'Why, that is a good sign, that my death is fast approaching; and, blessed be God, I can add, that my heart beats every day stronger and stronger for glory.'

"A few days before his dissolution, I found him sitting up in his arm chair, and scarcely able to move or speak. I addressed him very softly, and asked if his consolations continued to abound, as they had hitherto done? He quickly replied: 'O, my dear sir, it is impossible to describe how good God is to me. Since I have been sitting in this chair this afternoon (glory be to his name!), I have enjoyed such a season, such sweet communion with God, and such delightful manifestations of his presence with, and love to my soul, that it is impossible for words, or any language, to express them. I have had peace and joy unutterable; and I fear not, but that God's consolations and supports will continue.' But he immediately recollected himself, and added, 'What have I said? God may, to be sure, as a sovereign, hide his face and his smiles from me; however, I believe he will not; and if he should, yet still will I trust in him: I know I am safe and secure; for his love and his covenant are everlasting.'"

To a friend calling upon him a day or two before his death, he said, with hands clasped and eyes lifted up and filled with tears of the most evident joy, "O my dear sir, I cannot tell you the comforts I feel in my soul; they are past expression. The consolations of God to such an unworthy wretch are so abundant, that he leaves me nothing to pray for but a continuance of them. I enjoy a heaven already in my soul. My prayers are all converted into praise. Nevertheless, I do not forget that I am still in the body, and liable to all those distressing fears which are incident to human nature, when under temptation and without any sensible divine support. But so long as the presence of God continues with me in the degree I now enjoy it, I cannot but think that such a desponding frame is impossible." All this he spoke with an emphasis the most ardent that can be conceived.

To the same friend, conversing upon the subject of his sickness, he said, "Sickness is no affliction; pain no curse; death itself no dissolution."

All his conversations, as he approached nearer and nearer to his decease, seemed more and more happy and heavenly. He frequently called himself the happiest man in the world. "O!" said he, "how this soul of mine longs to be gone! Like a bird imprisoned in a cage, it longs to take its flight. O, that I had wings like a dove, then would I flee away to the realms of bliss, and be at rest for ever! O, that some guardian angel might be commissioned; for I long to be absent from this body, and to be with my Lord for ever." Being asked by a friend if he always enjoyed such manifestations, he answered, "I cannot say there are no intermissions; for, if there were not, my consolations would be more and greater than I could possibly bear; but when they abate, they leave such an abiding sense of God's goodness, and of the certainty of my being fixed upon the eternal rock Christ Jesus, that my soul is still filled with peace and joy."

At another time, and indeed for many days together, he cried out, "O, what a day of sunshine, has this been to me! I have not words to express it. It is unutterable. O, my friends, how good is God! almost without interruption, his presence has been with me." And then, repeating several passages of Scripture, he added, "What a great thing it is to rejoice in death!" Speaking of Christ, he said, "His love is unutterable!" He was happy in declaring that the 8TH chapter of the epistle to the Romans, from the 33RD to the end of the six following verses, were the joy and comfort of his soul. Upon that portion of Scripture he often descanted with great delight, and would be frequently ejaculating, "Lord Jesus! why tarriest thou so long!" He sometimes said, "I find as the bottles of heaven empty, they are filled again"; meaning, probably, the continual comforts of grace, which he abundantly enjoyed.

When he drew near his end, he said, waking from a slumber; "O, what delights! Who can fathom the joys of the third heaven?" And, a little before his departure, he was blessing and praising God for continuing to him his understanding in clearness; "but," added he in a rapture, "for what is most of all, his abiding presence, and the shining of his love upon my soul. The sky," said he, "is clear; there is no cloud: Come, Lord Jesus, come quickly!"

Within an hour of his death he called his friends and his servant, and asked them if they could give him up? Upon their answering in the affirmative, since it pleased the Lord to be so gracious to him, he replied; "O, what a blessing it is, you are made willing to give me up into the hands of my dear Redeemer, and to part with me: it will not be long before God takes me; for no mortal man can live," bursting, while he said it, into tears of joy, "after the glories which God has manifested to my soul." Soon after this he closed his eyes, and found (as Milton finely expresses it)

————"A death like sleep,
A gentle wafting to immortal life."

He died on Tuesday, August 11TH, 1778, in the 38TH year of his age.

While rehearsing these particulars, we cannot help laying down the pen to drop a tear to the revered memory of this highly respectable minister of Jesus Christ.———Yet a little time, and all painful recollections and sensations of this kind will be at an end, we shall have no more occasion to mark the vicissitudes of human affairs, nor to reflect on the nature and mixture of all earthly enjoyments; the sorrows of mortality shall never more be experienced, for the luster of all that is great and lovely in the human character will be absorbed in the presence and in the perfect fruition of the adorable Trinity.

On Monday, August 17TH, 1778, at four o'clock in the afternoon, his remains were brought from Knightsbridge to Tottenham Court Chapel, to be interred. Though the time was kept as private as possible, there were notwithstanding, several thousands of persons present at the solemnity. It was his particular request that no funeral sermon should be preached, as he desired to be laid in the tomb unnoticed and unregarded. He sought for no eulogium while living, and any panegyrics bestowed upon him when his course was run, he knew could be of no service, and that they are too often justly construed to proceed from pride, vanity, and weakness.

The Rev. Rowland Hill, prior to the burial service, could not refrain from trespassing upon the solicitation of his departed friend, by addressing the multitude on the solemn occasion, and embraced the opportunity of affectionately declaring the love and veneration he felt for the deceased. The beautiful simplicity of his pathos, and the incomparably exquisite sensibility he showed, were more than equivalent to the most studied harangue, furnished with all the trappings of meretricious ornaments. The funeral obsequies were read by Dr. Illingworth, and concluded with a suitable hymn. The casket which held this precious jewel now lies entombed in the family grave of Mr. Hussey, under the gallery opposite the pulpit in the above chapel, whereon is fixed a plain stone, with only his name and age inscribed. His clay tenement rests there until the morning of the resurrection, when the trump of God, and the voice of the archangel, shall call forth his sleeping dust to join the disembodied spirit, now in the realms of bliss and glory.

In commendation of his Hymns and Poems, we select the following opinion of James Montgomery. "The hymns of the Rev. Augustus Toplady form a striking contrast with the mild and humane tone of Doddridge's. There is a peculiarly etherial spirit in some of them; in which, whether mourning or rejoicing, praying or praising, the writer seems absorbed in the full triumph of faith, and, 'whether in the body or out of the body, caught up into the third heaven,' and beholding unutterable things. He evidently kindled his poetic torch at that of his contemporary, Charles Wesley; and, though inferior in breadth and volume of flame, yet the light which it sheds is not less vivid and sparkling, while it may be said to be more delicate to the eye, and refreshing to the spirits, than that prodigality of radiance which the rival luminary cast alike on everything it touched. 'Rock of ages, cleft for me,' etc., is well known and appreciated. 'Deathless principle, arise,' etc., is scarcely suitable to be sung; but it may be uttered by 'the dying Christian to his soul,' with a joy which he alone can feel, and feel only at the height, in the last moment of time, and the first of eternity. Had this poem appeared without a name, it might have been confidently set down as the production of Charles Wesley,—as one of Charles Wesley's loveliest progeny has been fathered upon Augustus Toplady: 'Christ, whose glory fills the skies,' etc." This just commendation of the Moravian bard will be *endorsed* by *every Christian* who is wont to make melody in his heart to the Lord.

The volume now presented to a Christian public contains:—first, a faithful reprint of the hymns which Mr. Toplady published in the year 1759.—Five of these, however, having been subsequently enlarged by the author, these latter versions are given in preference to the former more imperfect compositions. Secondly, the hymns which bear his well-known signature *"Minimus"* in the Gospel Magazine,[1] numbered 1–21, and composed between the years 1770–1776, with four others found elsewhere. The fine hymn, "Holy Ghost, dispel our sadness," although only altered from J. C. Jacobi's translation of Paul Gerhardt's hymn on the Holy Ghost, has been retained in this volume, as it is a version justly esteemed by many. Several hymns of different authors have been ascribed to Toplady,[2] but these were never claimed by him nor inserted in the volume of his published poems, and it was not till fourteen years after his death that the editor of his works inserted in the sixth volume some of Charles Wesley's finest hymns, together with the compositions of other authors, while he at the same time mutilated and omitted several hymns which embellish the pages of his own poems. It must therefore be satisfactory to possess, for the first time after the lapse of a century, a complete collection of all the hymns composed by the author of "Deathless principle," and the publisher has spared no pains to authenticate every hymn in the present volume, and to secure to the friends of English hymnody a correct reprint of the originals.

---

1 He became editor of this magazine in December 1775, but was compelled by illness to relinquish it in the following summer 1776. His articles often appeared under the modest signature of *'Minimus,'* though he sometimes adopted that of *"Concionator";* there are also a few papers with the initials of his own name.

2 A correct list of these hymns, with the names of the real authors, is given in this volume.

PREFACE

The following Pieces are not recommended to the Patronage of the Public on account of any excellency in *Themselves*, but merely for the Importance of their *Subjects:* for, however defective the *Superstructure* may be, it's *Foundation* is unquestionably good. All the Doctrines here advanced, deduce their Authority from the sacred Scriptures, and their faithful Epitome—the Homilies of the Established Church.

And that the Dignity of Truths so momentous might be impaired as little as possible by the manner of expressing them, they are often introduced in the *very Words* of the inspired Writers, and our venerable Reformers; as every Reader, who is intimate with the two invaluable Books just mentioned, cannot fail of observing.

Since all the *Essentials* of Religion are comprised in these two, Sound *Faith*, and a suitable course of *Obedience*, every thing that may give offense to Christians dissenting from each other in Points merely *indifferent*, is studiously avoided, and no particular Tenets any where struck at, except one or two, which apparently tend to invalidate the Authority of Revelation, and, by consequence, to subvert the whole Subject of Christianity.

The Author wishes it was in his Power to do justice to the Sublime Doctrines here treated of; but, 'till Death is swallowed up in Victory, the glorious Privileges and ineffable Benefits redounding to Believers from the Manifestation of God in the Flesh, cannot be perfectly *Conceived,* much less properly *Expressed.*

Lest a continued Sameness should *Pall*, and want of Method *Confuse* the Reader, the Metre is occasionally varied, and the whole presents itself to his View digested as follows:

1. Petitionary Hymns.
2. Hymns of Praise.
3. Paraphrases on some Select Portions of Holy Writ.
4. Hymns of Invitation.
5. A few Pieces occasioned by the Death of Friends.

And, Lastly, several Pieces not properly referable to any of the preceding Heads, thrown together by way of Appendix.

PETITIONARY HYMNS

Te Mente purâ et simplici
Te Voce, te Cantu pio,
Rogare curvato Genu,
Plendo et canendo discimus.—Prudentius.

Oratio est Oris Ratio, per quam intima Cordis
Nostri manifestamus Deo.

REFINING FULLER, MAKE ME CLEAN

Refining Fuller, make me clean,
  On me thy costly Pearl bestow:
Thou art thyself the Pearl I prize,
  The only Joy I seek below.

Disperse the Clouds that damp my Soul,
  And make my Heart unfit for thee:
Cast me not off, but Seal me now
  Thine own peculiar Property.

Look on the Wounds of CHRIST for me,
  My Sentence graciously Reprieve:
Extend thy peaceful Sceptre, LORD,
  And bid the dying Traitor Live.

Tho' I've transgress'd the Rules prescrib'd,
  And dar'd the Justice I adore,
Yet let thy smiling Mercy say,
  Depart in Peace, and sin no more.

AT ENTERING INTO THE CHURCH

Father of Love, to thee I bend
  My Heart, and lift mine Eyes;
Let now my Pray'r and Praise ascend
  As Odours to the Skies.

Thy pard'ning Voice I come to hear,
  To know thee as thou art:
Thy Ministers can reach the Ear,
  But thou must touch the Heart.

O stamp me in thy Heavenly Mould,
  And grant thy Word apply'd
May bring forth Fruit an hundred Fold,
  And speak me justify'd.

WHEN SERVICE IS ENDED

Lord, let me not thy Courts depart,
  Nor quit thy Mercy-seat
Before I feel thee in my Heart,
  And there the Saviour meet.

Water the seed in Weakness sown,
  And evermore improve;
Make me a Garden of thine own,
  My ev'ry Flow'r be Love!

O send my Soul in Peace away;
  For both my Lord hath bought:
And let my Heart, exulting, say,
  I've found the Pearl I sought!

FOR THE MORNING

JESUS, by whose Grace I live
From the fear of Evil kept,
Thou hast lengthen'd my Reprieve,
Held in Being while I slept;
With the Day my Heart renew;
Let me wake thy Will to do.

Since the last revolving Dawn
Scattered the Nocturnal Cloud,
O how many Souls have gone,
Unprepar'd, to meet their GOD!
Yet thou dost prolong my Breath,
Hast not seal'd my Eyes in Death.

O that I may keep thy Word,
Taught by thee to Watch and Pray!
To thy Service, dearest LORD,
Sanctify th' ensuing Day:
Swift its fleeting Moments haste;
Doom'd, perhaps, to be my Last.

Crucified to all below,
Earth shall never be my Care:
Wealth and Honour I forego;
This my only Wish and Care
Thine in Life and Death to be,
Now and to Eternity.

FOR THE EVENING

God of Love, whose Truth and Grace
   Reach unbounded as the Skies,
Hear thy Creature's feeble Praise;
   Let my Ev'ning Sacrifice
Mount as Incense to thy Throne,
On the Merits of thy Son.

Me thy Providence has led
   Through another busy Day;
Over me thy Wings were spread,
   Chasing Sin and Death away:
Thou hast been my faithful Shield,
Thou my Footsteps hast upheld.

Tho' the sable Veil of Night
   Hides the cheering Face of Heav'n,
Let me triumph in the Sight
   Of my Guilt in Thee forgiv'n;
In my Heart the Witness feel,
See the great Invisible.

I will lay me down to sleep,
   Sweetly take my rest in Thee,
Ev'ry Moment brought a Step
   Nearer to Eternity:
I shall soon from Earth ascend,
Quickly reach my Journey's End.

All my Sins imputed were
   To my dear, incarnate God;
Bury'd in his Grave they are,
   Drown'd in his atoning Blood:

Me thou can'st not now condemn,
Righteous and complete in him.

In the Saviour's Right I claim
    All the Blessings he hath bought;
For my Soul the dying Lamb
    Hath a full Redemption wrought:
Heav'n, through his Desert, is mine;
CHRIST'S I am, and CHRIST is thine!

THERE IS MERCY WITH THEE

LORD, should'st thou weigh my Righteousness,
Or mark what I have done amiss,
How should thy Servant stand?
Tho' others might, yet surely I
Must hide my Face, nor dare to cry
For mercy at thy Hand.

But thou art loth thy Bolts to shoot;
Backward and slow to execute
The Vengeance due to me:
Thou dost not willingly reprove,
For all the mild Effects of Love
Are center'd, LORD, in thee.

O may I grasp the golden Fruit,
Nor tread the Mercy under Foot,
Which fain would make me thine;
Nor ever wander from thy Path,
Or re-incur that dreadful Wrath,
Thou would'st not should be mine!

Shine, then, thou all-subduing Light,
The Pow'rs of Darkness put to Flight,
Nor from me ever part:
From Earth to Heav'n be thou my Guide;
And O, above each Gift beside,
Give me a perfect Heart!

IN SICKNESS

Jesus, since I with thee am one,
  Confirm my Soul in thee,
And still continue to tread down
  The Man of Sin in me.

Let not the Enemy prevail
  In this my feeble Hour:
O Frustrate all the Hopes of Hell,
  Redeem from Satan's Pow'r.

Arm me, O Lord, from Head to Foot
  With Righteousness Divine:
My Soul in Jesus firmly root,
  And seal the Saviour mine.

Proportion'd to my Pains below,
  O let my Joys increase,
And Mercy to my Spirit flow
  In healing Streams of Peace.

In Life and Death be thou my God,
  And I am more than safe:
Smite me with thy paternal Rod,
  Support me with thy Staff.

Lay on me, Saviour, what thou wilt,
  But give me Strength to bear:
Thy gracious Hand this Cross hath dealt
  Which cannot be severe.

As Gold refin'd may I come out.
  In Sorrow's Furnace try'd;
Preserv'd from Faithlessness and Doubt,
  And soundly purify'd.

When, overwhelm'd with sore Distress,
Out of the Pit I cry,
On JESUS suffering in my Place,
Help me to fix mine Eye:

When[1] marr'd with Tears and Blood and Sweat,
The godlike Sufferer lay,
And, in my stead, sustain'd the Heat
And Burthen of the Day.

The Pangs which my weak Nature knows
Are swallow'd up in thine:
How numberless thy pond'rous Woes,
How few, how light are mine!

O might I learn of thee to bear
Temptation, Pain and Loss!
Give me an Heart inur'd to Prayer,
And fitted to the Cross.

Make me, O LORD, thy patient son;
Thy Language mine shall be:
"Father, thy gracious will be done,
"I take the Cup from thee."

While thus my Soul is fixt on Him
Once fasten'd to the Wood,
Safe shall I pass through *Jordan's* Stream
And reach the Realms of God.

And when my Soul mounts up to keep
With thee the Marriage Feast,
I shall not *die*, but *fall asleep*
On my Redeemer's Breast.

1 Referring to his Agony in the Garden.

HE DWELLETH WITH YOU AND SHALL BE IN YOU

Even the Spirit of truth; whom the world cannot receive, because it seeth him not, neither knoweth him: but ye know him; for he dwelleth with you, and shall be in you.—John 14:17.

Saviour, I thy Word believe,
My Unbelief remove;
Now thy quick'ning Spirit give,
The unction from above;
Show me, Lord, how good thou art,
My Soul with all thy Fullness fill:
Send the Witness, in my Heart
The Holy Ghost reveal.

Dead in Sin 'till then I lie,
Bereft of Pow'r to rise;
'Till thy Spirit inwardly
Thy saving Blood applies:
Now the mighty Gift impart,
My Sin erase, my Pardon seal;
Send the Witness, in my Heart
The Holy Ghost reveal.

Blessed Comforter, come down,
And Live and Move in me;
Make my ev'ry Deed thine own,
In all Things led by thee:
Bid my ev'ry Lust depart,
And with me O vouchsafe to dwell;
Faithful Witness, in my Heart
Thy perfect Light reveal.

Let me in thy Love rejoice,
Thy Shrine, thy pure Abode;

Tell me, by thine inward Voice,
  That I'm a Child of God:
Lord, I chuse the better Part,
  Jesus, I wait thy Peace to feel;
Send the Witness, in my Heart
  The Holy Ghost reveal.

Whom the World cannot receive,
  O manifest in me:
Son of God, I cease to live
  When I am not in Thee;
Now impute thy whole Desert,
  Restore the Joy from whence I fell:
Breathe the Witness, in my Heart
  The Holy Ghost reveal.

Hast thou not for Sinners groan'd,
  And all Men dearly bought?
Saviour, be in Mercy found
  Of those that seek thee not:
Scatter round thy keenest Darts,
  And Sin from every Soul expel;
Send the Witness, in their Hearts
  The Holy Ghost reveal.

FOR THE KING OF PRUSSIA

Great God, whom Heav'n and Earth and Sea,
With all their countless Hosts, obey,
Upheld by whom the Nations stand,
And Empires fall at thy Command:

Still to thy chosen *Gideon* prove
A Wall of Fire, a Shield of Love;
Him in their Hands let Angels bear,
And screen Him in the Day of War.

Long may he stand, as now he does,
The Bulwark of thy People's Cause;
Let *France* and *Austria* weep in Blood,
Just Victims to the Sword of God.

Humble, by Him, their haughty Boast,
And lay their Glory in the Dust;
Give Him to make thy Fury known,
And mow their proud Battalions down.

Beneath thy long suspended Ire
Let papal Antichrist expire;
Thy Knowledge spread from Sea to Sea,
'Till ev'ry Nation bows to Thee.

Then show thyself the Prince of Peace,
Make Hell-born Enmity to cease;
All with thy sacred Love inspire,
And burn their Chariots in the Fire.

In sunder knap each hostile Spear;
Let all the Saviour's Liv'ry wear;
The universal Sabbath prove,
The utmost Rest of Christian Love!

The World shall then no Discord know,
But Hand in Hand to *Canaan* go,
JESUS, the peaceful King, adore,
And learn the Art of War no more.

DESIRING TO BE GIVEN UP TO GOD

O that my Heart was right with thee,
  And lov'd thee with a perfect Love!
O that my LORD would dwell in me,
  And never from his Seat remove!
JESUS, take off th' impending Load,
And set my Soul on Fire for GOD!

Thou seest I grope in endless Night
  Until thou in my Heart appear;
Kindle the Flame, O LORD, and light
  Thine everlasting Candle there:
Thy Presence puts the Shadows by;
If thou art gone, how dark am I!

Ah! LORD, how should thy Servant see,
  Unless thou give me seeing Eyes?
Well may I fall, if out of Thee;
  If out of thee, How should I rise?
I wander, LORD, without thy Aid,
And lose my Way in Midnight Shade.

Thy Light O send me from above,
  All other Lights are nothing worth;
Light up in me the Lamp of Love
  To guide me through this Labrynth Earth;
Nor let the impious Breath of Doubt
Ever draw near to put it out.

Thy bright, unerring Light afford,
  A Light that gives the Sinner Hope;
And from the House of Bondage, LORD,
  O bring the weary Captive up;

Thine Hand alone can set me free:
And reach my Pardon out to me.

O let my Prayer Acceptance find,
   And bring the mighty Blessing down;
With Eye-salve, LORD, anoint the Blind,
   And seal me thine adopted Son:
A fallen, helpless Creature take,
And Heir of thy Salvation make.

LORD, SAVE US, WE PERISH!

(Matthew 8:25)

Pilot of the Soul, awake,
Save us for thy Mercy's Sake;
Now rebuke the angry Deep,
Save, O save thy sinking Ship!

Stand at the Helm, our Vessel steer,
Mighty on our Side appear;
Saviour, teach us to descry
Where the Rocks and Quicksands lie.

The Waves shall impotently roll,
If thou'rt the Anchor of the Soul:
At thy Word the Winds shall cease,
Storms be hush'd to perfect Peace.

Be thou our Haven of Retreat,
A Rock to fix our wav'ring Feet;
Teach us to own thy sov'reign Sway,
Whom the Winds and Seas obey.

O THAT MY WAYS WERE MADE SO DIRECT

O that my ways were made so strait,
And that the Lamp of Faith
Would, as a Star, direct my Feet
To find the narrow Path!

O that thy Strength might enter now,
And in my Heart abide,
To make me as a faithful Bow
That never starts aside!

O that I all to CHRIST were giv'n,
(From Sin and Earth set free)
Who kindly laid aside his Heav'n,
And gave Himself for me!

Not more the panting Hart desires
The cool, refreshing Stream,
Than my dry, thirsty Soul aspires
At being one with Him.

Set up thine Image in my Heart;
There let thy Kingdom come;
Bid ev'ry Idol now depart
Thy Temple and thy Home.

Still keep me in the heav'nly Path;
Bestow the inward Light;
And lead me by the Hand 'till Faith
Is ripened into Sight.

FATHER, TO THEE IN CHRIST I FLY

Father, to Thee in Christ I fly;
What tho' my Sins of Crimson Dye
  For thy Resentment Call?
My Crimes He did on *Calv'ry* bear,
The Blood that flow'd for Sinners there
  Shall cleanse me from them all.

Spirit divine, Thy Pow'r bring in;
O raise me from this Depth of Sin,
  Take off my guilty Load:
Now let me live through JESUS' Death,
And being justify'd by Faith,
  May I have Peace with GOD!

LORD, let me love thee e'er I die;
Tell me that with thy Saints, ev'n I
  Shall sing thy praise in Heav'n:
My Mourning into Joy convert,
And bind thou up a broken Heart
  That groans to be forgiv'n.

Foul as I am, and ripe for Hell,
Thou canst not from thy Throne repel
  A Soul that leans on GOD:
My Sins, at thy Command, shall be
Cast as a Stone into the Sea—
  The Sea of JESUS' Blood.

SUPREME HIGH PRIEST, THE PILGRIM'S LIGHT

Supreme high Priest, the Pilgrim's Light,
My Heart for Thee prepare,
Thine Image stamp and deeply write
Thy Superscription there.

Ah! let my Forehead bear thy Seal,
My Arm thy Badge retain,
My Heart the inward Witness feel
That I am born again.

Thy Peace, O Saviour, shed abroad,
That ev'ry Want supplies:
Then from its Guilt my Soul, renew'd,
Shall, Phoenix-like, arise.

Into thy humble Mansion come,
Set up thy Dwelling here;
Possess my Heart, and leave no Room
For Vice to harbour there.

Ah! give me, LORD, the single Eye
Which aims at nought but thee:
I fain would live, and yet not I—
Let JESUS live in me.

Like *Noah's* Dove, no Rest I find
But in thy Ark of Peace:
Thy Cross the Balance of my Mind,
Thy Wounds my Hiding-Place.

In vain the Tempter spreads the Snare,
If thou my Keeper art:
Get thee behind me, GOD is near,
My Saviour takes my Part!

On Him my Spirit I recline
Who put my Nature on;
His Light shall in my Darkness shine,
And guide me to his Throne

Him my Deliv'rer still I prove,
From Satan's ev'ry Art;
A precious Pearl, an inbred Love
Enshrin'd within my Heart.

O That the penetrating Sight
And Eagle's Eye were mine!
Undazzled at the boundless Light,
I'd see his Glory shine!

Ev'n now, by Faith, I see him live
To Crown the Conqu'ring Few;
Nor let me linger here, but strive
To gain the Prize in View.

Add, Saviour, to the Eagle's Eye
The Dove's aspiring Wing,
To bear me upwards to the Sky,
Thy Praises there to sing!

SELF-DEDICATION

Enter, JESUS, fill my Heart
With nothing else but Thee;
Now thy saving Pow'r exert,
And more than conquer Me:
Each intruding Rival kill
That hinders or obstructs thy Reign;
All thy glorious Might reveal,
And make me pure within.

Through my Soul in Mercy shine,
Thine Holy Spirit give;
Let Him witness, Lord, with mine
That I in JESUS live;
Set me free from Satan's Load,
The Gift of Liberty dispense:
In my Heart O shed abroad
Thy quick'ning Influence.

O that not a future Word,
Or Act, or Thought of mine
Might offend my gracious LORD,
Or quench the Light divine!
Take me, Saviour, as I am,
Self-will'd, unholy and unclean:
Stamp thy Likeness, write thy Name
Indelibly within.

Use the Gifts bestow'd on me
To thy great Praise alone;
LORD, the Talents lent by thee
Are thine and not my own:

May I in thy Service spend
  All the Graces thou hast giv'n,
Taken up, when Time shall end,
  To Live and Reign in Heav'n.

IN TEMPTATION

Compass'd by the Foe, on thee
  Feebly I presume to call;
Get thyself the Victory,
  Hold me and I shall not fall:
On thy Creature Mercy shew,
Thine I am by Purchase too.

Guard of my defenceless Heart,
  Wherefore hidest thou thy Face?
Mercy's Fountain Head thou art,
  Ever full of Truth and Grace:
Quell the roaring Lion's pow'r;
Father, save me from this Hour!

Sun of Righteousness, arise,
  Shed thy blissful Rays on me;
Kindly listen to my Cries,
  Try'd by Him who tempted Thee:
Thou my helpless Soul defend,
Keep me blameless to the End.

Rise in Vengeance from thy Seat;
  JESUS, LORD, make haste to save;
Me, to sift my Soul as Wheat,
  Satan hath desir'd to have:
Let Him not too far prevail,
Suffer not my Faith to fail.

Try'd, afflicted and distrest,
  By Temptation's searching Flame,
Tho', beneath its load opprest,
  Now in Heaviness I am,

I shall soon at Freedom be,
More than Conqueror in thee.

This Affliction shall work out,
  (Light and transient as it is)
When I am to *Sion* brought,
  Everlasting Joy and Peace:
Here but for a Moment try'd,
There for ever glorify'd.

O MAY I NEVER REST

O may I never rest
'Till I find Rest in Thee,
'Till, of my Pardon here possest,
I feel thy Love to me!

Unseal my darkened Eyes,
My fetter'd feet unbind;
The Lame shall, when thou say'st "arise,"
Run swifter than the Hind.

O draw the Alien near,
Bend the obdurate Neck;
O melt the Flint into a Tear,
And teach the Dumb to speak:

Turn not thy Face away,
Thy Look can make me clean;
Me in thy wedding Robe array,
And cover all my Sin.

Tell me, my GOD, for whom
Thy precious Blood was shed;
For Sinners? LORD, as such I come,
For such the Saviour bled:

Then raise a fallen Wretch,
Display thy Grace in me;
I am not out of Mercy's Reach,
Nor too far gone for thee.

Thou quickly wilt forgive,
My LORD will not delay;
JESUS, to Thee the time I leave,
And wait th' accepted Day:

I now rejoice in Hope
That I shall be made clean;
Thy Grace shall surely lift me up,
Above the Reach of Sin.

Hast thou not dy'd for me,
And call'd me from below?
O help me to lay Hold on Thee,
And ne'er to let Thee go!

Through ev'ry thorny Path
My Saviour I'll pursue:
A while submit to bear his Wrath,
Then share his Glory too.

FROM JUSTICE'S CONSUMING FLAME

From Justice's consuming Flame,
Saviour, I fly to thee:
O Look not on me as I am,
But as I fain would be.

Deserted in the Way I lie,
No Cure for me is found;
Thou good *Samaritan* pass by,
And bind up ev'ry Wound.

O may I, in the final Day,
At thy Right Hand appear!
Take now my Sins out of the Way,
Who did'st the Burthen bear.

Why should I thus a Rebel be,
And lose my dear-bought Crown?
O may I yield myself to thee,
And lay my Weapons down!

What tho' the fiery Serpent's bite
Hath poison'd ev'ry Vein—
I'll not Despair, but keep in Sight
The Wounds of JESUS slain.

My Soul thou wilt from Death retrieve,
For Sorrow grant me Joy:
Thy Pow'r is mightier to save
Than Satan's to destroy.

AFTER BEING SURPRISED INTO SIN

Ah! give me, LORD, myself to see,
  Against myself to Watch and Pray:
How weak am I, when left by Thee!
  How frail, how apt to fall away!
If but a Moment thou withdraw,
That Moment sees me break thy Law.

JESUS, the Sinner's only Trust,
  Let me now feel thy Grace infus'd;
Ah! raise a Captive from the Dust,
  Nor break a Reed already bruis'd!
Visit me, LORD, in Peace again,
Nor let me seek thy Face in vain.

How have I forc'd thee from my Heart,
  And trampled on thy mild Commands!
Loving to ev'ry Man thou art,
  My Friend and Saviour, for there stands
Betwixt thy Love and Me no Screen,
But what my Sins have put between.

O bury these, and let me find
  Peace and Salvation in thy Name;
Be Thou the Eyesight of the Blind,
  The Staff and Ancles of the Lame,
My lifter up whene'er I fall,
My Strength, my Portion and my All!

Let thy meek Mind descend on me,
  Thy Holy Spirit from above:
Assist me Lord, to follow Thee,
  Drawn by th' endearing Cords of Love,

Made perfect by thy cleansing Blood,
Completely sav'd and born of God.

Renew my desecrated Heart,
To Sinless purity restore;
Cause me to act a faithful Part
And grieve thy pitying Love no more;
And, when my Race on Earth is run,
To fly in Triumph to thy Throne.

CHRIST THE LIGHT OF HIS PEOPLE[1]

I lift my Heart and Eyes to Thee,
  JESUS, Thou unextinguish'd Light:
My guardian stay and Leader be,
  My Cloud by Day, my Fire by Night.

Glory of Israel, shine within;
  Unshadow'd, uneclips'd appear:
With Beams of Grace exhale my Sin;
  Break forth, thou bright and morning Star.

The World a trackless Labrynth is,
  Be thou my Thread and faithful Clue;
Thy Kingdom and thy righteousness
  The only Objects I pursue.

Light of the Gentiles, Thee I hail;
  Essential Truth, thyself impart!
Spirit of Light, his Face reveal;
  And set thy Signet on my Heart.

Thy office 'tis t' enlighten man,
  And point him to the heav'nly Prize;
The hidden Things of God t' explain,
  And shine the Darkness from our Eyes.

Witness of Christ within my Heart,
  My Int'rest in his Love display;
My Int'rest in that better Part,
  Which never can be torn away.

In bondage 'till thou set me free,
  Fain would I know my part in Him;

1 This hymn was revised in after years. We give the later version.

The Brightness of his Rising see,
And bask in thy meridian Beam.

Shine then thou uncreated Ray!
If but a Moment Thou withdraw,
That Moment sees me go astray,
That Moment sees me break thy Law.

The Word and Spirit both conspire
To tell thy Church she is forgiv'n;
And lift her daily high'r and high'r,
'Till all her Joys are crown'd with Heav'n.

To that bless'd Realm of bright Repose,
Thou wilt conduct my weary Feet;
Where Peace no interruption knows,
And where my Sun shall never set.

CHAINED TO THE WORLD, TO SIN TIED DOWN

Chained to the World, to Sin ty'd down,
In Darkness still I lie;
Lord, break my Bonds, Lord, give me Wings,
And teach me how to fly.

Instruct my feeble Hands to War,
In me thy Strength reveal,
To put my ev'ry Lust to Death,
And fight thy Battles well.

Rend ev'ry Veil that shades thy Face,
Put on thine Helmet, Lord:
My Sin shall fall, my Guilt expire
Beneath thy conqu'ring Sword.

Thou art the Mighty God of Hosts,
Whose Counsels never fail;
Be thou my glorious Chief, and then
I cannot but prevail.

Then slay my Sins without Reserve,
Burn up each Lust in me;
Kill, kill my vain rebellious Heart,
And I shall live to Thee.

O WHEN WILT THOU MY SAVIOUR BE?

O when wilt thou my Saviour be?
  O when shall I be clean,
The true, eternal Sabbath see,
  A perfect Rest from Sin?

JESUS, the Sinner's Rest thou art
  From Guilt and Fear and Pain;
While thou art absent from my Heart
  I look for Rest in vain.

The Consolations of thy Word
  My Soul have long upheld;
The faithful Promise of the Lord
  Shall surely be fulfill'd:

I look to my incarnate GOD,
  'Till he his Work begin,
And wait 'till his redeeming Blood
  Shall cleanse me from all Sin.

His great Salvation I shall know,
  And perfect Liberty;
Onward to Sin he cannot go,
  Whoe'er abides in Thee:

Added to the Redeemer's Fold,
  I shall in him rejoice;
I all his Glory shall behold,
  And hear my Shepherd's Voice.

O that I now the voice might hear
  That speaks my Sins forgiv'n!
His Word is past to give me *here*
  The inward Pledge of Heav'n:

His Blood shall over all prevail,
  And sanctify th' Unclean;
The Grace that saves from future Hell
  Shall save from present Sin.

A PRAYER IN BEHALF OF THE ARIANS

My yielding Heart dissolves as Wax
By penetrating Fire subdu'd,
Whenever my Beloved speaks,
And wooes me to be one with God.

The Language of redeeming Love,
In dying Eloquence exprest,
Hath forc'd my backward Heart to prove
The sweetness of his People's Rest.

Jesus, who would stand off from Thee,
Proudly thy proffer'd Heav'n refuse?
Despise the glorious Liberty,
Thy mercy bids them freely use?

Saviour, how long shall men Blaspheme,
And trample on their dying God?
From faithless Pride O rescue them,
And save them by thy slighted Blood!

Let all confess and own with me,
That thou art sweet, thy Burden light:
O give them Eyes to look to Thee,
And wash their spotted Garments white.

Thy Blood's the Jordan of the Soul
That does away the Guilt of Sin:
Let all wash there, and all are whole,
Each lep'rous Naaman shall be clean.

O Jesus, manifest thy Grace,
Scatter thy mighty Darts abroad;
Constrain the unbelieving Race
To fall before a wounded God.

Why should they dye, whom thou hast bought,
With horrid unbelief enflam'd?
Yet die they must, (tremendous Thought!)
For thou hast said they shall be damn'd.

Thee, perfect GOD and perfect Man,
O let them, e'er too late, confess:
Why should they slay their Lord again,
And sink to Hell as none of His?

May they be brought that Truth to see
Thy Spirit inwardly reveals;
Convinc'd, O Saviour, that in Thee
The Fulness of the Godhead dwells!

O that they might, in Time, disclaim
Their horrid Plea and black Design,
And know there is no other Name,
Whereby they may be Sav'd, but thine!

Them, dead in Trespasses and Sins,
Quicken, renew, and make alive:
Confirm the whole, the Lepers cleanse,
Each dying Soul let CHRIST revive.

Thy Hands, thy Side, thy Feet were pierc'd
The most Unholy to restore:
Thy Blood was shed to heal the Worst,
And save the poorest of the Poor.

Then let them taste thy saving Grace,
Be cleans'd and glorified by thee;
And in the Sacrifice of Praise
Employ a blest Eternity.

JESUS, THY LIGHT IMPART

JESUS, thy Light impart,
And lead me in thy Path:
I have an unbelieving Heart,
But thou can'st give me Faith.

The Work in me fulfil
Which mercy hath begun;
I have a proud, rebellious Will,
But thou can'st melt it down.

Sin on my Heart is wrote;
I am throughout impure:
But my Disease, O LORD, is not
Too hard for thee to cure.

The Darkness of my Mind
Lies open to thy Sight;
JESUS, I am, by nature, blind,
But thou can'st give me Light.

Send down thy Holy Ghost
To cleanse and fill with Peace;
For O mine inward Parts, thou know'st,
Are very Wickedness.

Thy Love all Power hath,
It's Pow'r in me exert,
And give me living, active Faith
That purifies the Heart.

Unrivall'd reign within,
My only Sovereign be;
O crucify the Man of Sin,
And form thyself in Me.

Thy Blood's renewing Might
Can make the foulest clean,
Can wash the Ethiopian white,
And change the Leopard's Skin:

That, that can bring me nigh,
And wipe my Sins away,
Can lift my abject Soul on high,
And call me into Day.

Fulfil thy gracious Word,
And shew my Guilt forgiv'n,
Bid me embrace my dying Lord,
And mount with Him to Heav'n.

THE BELIEVER'S WISH[1]

Empty'd of Earth I fain would be,
Of Sin, Myself, and all but THEE;
Only reserv'd for Christ that died,
Surrender'd to the Crucified:

Sequester'd from the Noise and Strife,
The Lust, the Pomp, and Pride of Life;
For Heav'n alone my Heart prepare,
And have my Conversation there.

Nothing, save Jesus, would I know;
My Friend and my Companion THOU!
Lord, seize my Heart, assert thy right,
And put all other loves to flight.

The Idols tread beneath thy Feet,
And to Thyself the Conquest get:
Let Sin no more oppose my Lord,
Slam by thy Spirit's two-edg'd Sword.

Compel my Soul thy sway to own;
Self-will, self-righteousness dethrone:
Let Dagon fall before thy Face,
The Ark remaining in its place.

Detach, from sublunary joys,
One that would only hear Thy voice,
Thy Beauty see, thy Grace admire,
Nor glow but with celestial Fire!

Larger Communion let me prove
With Thee, blest object of my love;

---

1 This hymn was revived in after years; the latter version.

But, O, for this no pow'r have I;
My strength is at thy Feet to lie.

Fain would I mount, fain would I glow,
And loose my Cable from below:
But I can only spread my Sail;
Thou, Thou must breathe th' auspicious Gale!

At Anchor laid, remote from Home,
Toiling I cry, Sweet Spirit come!
Celestial Breeze, no longer stay,
But swell my Sails, and speed my Way.

Open my Heart; the Key is thine:
My Will effectually incline:
Possess a Soul, that fain would be,
Lord, only intimate with Thee.

BEFORE MEAT

Whether therefore ye eat, or drink, or whatsoever ye do, do all to the glory of God.—1 CORINTHIANS 10:31.

LORD, we invite Thee here,
Vouchsafe to be our Guest;
JESUS, do thou appear,
The Master of the Feast:
Thy quick'ning Presence let us prove,
And banquet on thy hidden Love.

With Manna from on high
Feed thine Inheritance,
And come and Sanctify
Our outward Sustenance:
With it the inward Food be giv'n,
The Bread of Life, the Wine of Heav'n.

FOR THE MORNING

My Soul, can'st thou no higher rise
To meet thy God, than this?
Yet, Lord, accept my Sacrifice,
Defective as it is.

Tune all my Organs to thy Praise,
The Psalmist's Muse impart;
And, with thy penetrating Rays,
O melt my frozen Heart.

Give me Thyself the only Good,
And ever with me stay,
Whose faithful Mercies are renew'd
With each returning Day.

All! guide me with a Father's Eye,
Nor from my Soul depart,
But let the Day Star from on High
Illuminate my Heart.

This Day preserve me without Sin,
Unspotted in thy Ways;
And hear me, while I usher in
The welcome Dawn with Praise.

Far as the East from West remove
Each earthly, vain Desire;
And raise me on the Wings of Love,
'Till I can mount no higher.

FOR THE EVENING

Thou unexhausted Mine of Bliss,
   From whence all Comfort flows,
Inspire me with that Holy Peace
   Which none but Virtue knows:

The Curtains of thy Love extend
   Around my calm Abode;
As I began so may I end
   My ev'ry Day with God.

My Life unhurt thine Hand hath kept,
   Accept the Praise I pay
For all the Dangers I've escap'd,
   And Mercies of the Day.

Far, far away the Tempter chase,
   My Soul from Terror keep;
Let Angels fill this hallow'd Place
   And guard me as I sleep.

O wash out ev'ry Sin whereby,
   This Day, I have transgrest;
And seal my Pardon e'er I give
   My slumb'ring Eye-lids Rest:

Prepare me for the Bed of Death;
   Be that my hourly Thought,
That, sleeping and awake, my Soul
   May be without a Spot.

HE IS THE PROPITIATION FOR OUR SINS

O Thou that hear'st the Prayer of Faith,
Wilt thou not save a Soul from Death
  That casts itself on Thee?
I have no Refuge of my own,
But fly to what my Lord hath done
  And suffer'd once for Me.

Slain in the guilty Sinner's stead,
His spotless Righteousness I plead,
  And his availing Blood:
Thy Merit, Lord, my Robe shall be,
Thy Merit shall atone for me,
  And bring me near to God.

Then snatch me from eternal Death,
The Spirit of Adoption breathe,
  His Consolation send;
By Him some Word of Life impart,
And sweetly whisper to my Heart,
  "Thy Maker is thy Friend."

The King of Terrors *then* would be
A welcome Messenger to me,
  That bids me come away:
Unclog'd by Earth or earthly Things,
I'd mount upon his sable Wings
  To everlasting Day.

FOR THE EARTH SHALL BE FILLED

For the earth shall be filled with the knowledge of the glory of the LORD, as the waters cover the sea.—HABAKKUK 2:14.

Bring thy Kingdom, LORD, make haste,
  Bring on the glorious Day,
From the Greatest to the Least
  When all shall own thy Sway:
When the Convert World with Grief,
  Shall see the Error of their Ways,
Lay aside their Unbelief,
  And yield to dying Grace.

In thy Gospel-Chariot, Lord,
  Drive through Earth's utmost Bound;
Spread the Odour of thy Word
  Through all the Nations round:
Fill the darken'd Earth with Light,
  Thine own victorious Cause advance;
Take the Heathen as the Right
  Of thine Inheritance.

In our Day expose to view
  The standard of the Lamb;
Bid the Nations flock thereto
  Who never knew thy Name:
Let them quit the downward Road,
  Compell'd thy saying to receive;
Turn'd from Satan unto God,
  With one consent Believe.

O that all who know thee not,
  Or, knowing, wont submit,
Whom thy dying Love hath bought,
  Might fall and kiss thy Feet!

O that all Mankind might taste
  Thy Mercy, and thy Subjects be!
And, my God, among the rest,
  Reign absolute in Me!

REDEEMER, WHITHER SHOULD I FLEE

Redeemer, whither should I flee,
  Or how escape the Wrath to come?
The weary Sinner flies to Thee
  For Shelter from impending Doom:
Smile on me, dearest LORD, and shew
Thyself the friend of Sinners now.

Beneath the shadow of thy Cross
  My heavy-laden Soul finds Rest:
Let me esteem the World as Dross
  So I may be of Thee possest!
I borrow ev'ry Joy from Thee,
For thou art Life and Light to me.

Close to my Saviour's bloody Tree
  My Soul, untir'd, shall ever cleave;
Both scourg'd and crucify'd with Thee,
  With CHRIST resolved to die and live:
My Pray'r, my great Ambition this,
Living and dying, to be his.

O nail me to the sacred Wood,
  There tie me with thy Spirit's Chain;
There seal me with thy fast'ning Blood,
  Nor ever let me loose again:
There let me bow my suppliant Knee,
And own no other LORD but Thee!

LORD, STAND NOT OFF, COME NEARER STILL

LORD, stand not off, come nearer still,
Illuminate my darken'd Soul:
Renew my Heart, correct my Will,
Make the polluted Leper whole.

Behold my Struggles, LORD, and set
My Sin-bound Soul at Liberty:
Lend me thine Hand to break the Net,
And bid the fetter'd Slave be Free.

My own Desert I cannot plead,
My purest Silver is but Dross:
Let JESU's Merits intercede;
O nail my Errors to his Cross.

Fain would I mount to Thee my Crown,
And gain the Realms of endless Light;
But fett'ring Earth still keeps me down,
And Sin impediates my Flight.

Father, to me impart thy Bread,
To me thine healing Manna give:
On Life eternal let me feed,
That my diseased Soul may live.

Unworthy to *intreat* thy Grace,
Unworthier still thy Grace t' *obtain,*
I plead my Surety's Righteousness,
Nor shall my plea be urg'd in vain.

WHERE TWO OR THREE ARE GATHERED TOGETHER IN MY NAME

JESUS, God of Love, attend,
From thy glorious Throne descend;
Answer now some waiting Heart,
Now some harden'd Soul convert:
To our Advocate we fly,
Let us feel IMMANUEL nigh;
Manifest thy Love abroad,
Make us now the Sons of GOD.

Hover round us, King of Kings,
Rise with Healing in thy Wings;
Melt our Obstinacy down,
Force us to become thine own:
Set, O set the Captives free,
Draw our backward Souls to Thee,
Let us all from Thee receive
Light to see and Life to live.

Prostrate at thy Mercy Seat
Let us our Beloved meet,
Give us in thyself a Part
Deep engraven on thine Heart:
Let us hear thy pard'ning Voice,
Bid the broken Bones rejoice;
Condemnation do away,
O make this the perfect Day!

Father, Son and Holy Ghost,
Join to seek and save the Lost:
Raise some Sinner to thy Throne,
Add a Jewel to thy Crown!
Are we not, without thy Light,

Darken'd with Egyptian Night?
Light of Light, thy Pow'r exert,
Lighten each benighted Heart!

PART II.

Pray'r can Mercy's Door unlock;
Open, Lord, to us that knock!
Us the Heirs of Glory seal,
With thy Benediction fill:
Holy Spirit make us His,
Visit ev'ry Soul in Peace;
Force our vanquish'd Hearts to say,
Love Divine has won the Day!

Give the heavy-laden Rest,
CHRIST make known in ev'ry Breast;
Void of Thee we quickly die;
Turn our Sackcloth into Joy:
Witness all our Sins forgiv'n,
Grant on Earth a Glimpse of Heav'n:
Bring the joyful Tidings down,
Fit us for our destin'd Crown.

Let us chaunt melodious Hymns,
Loud as those of Cherubims;
Join with Heart and Tongue to bless
CHRIST our Strength and Righteousness:
All our Praise to him belongs,
Theme of our sublimest Songs;
Object of our choicest Love,
Thee we laud with Hosts above.

Thee we hail with joint Acclaim,
Shout the Glories of thy Name;

Ever may we feel Thee thus,
Dear IMMANUEL, GOD with us!
Prince of Peace, thy People see,
All our Thanks we aim at Thee;
Deign our Tribute to receive,
Praise is all we have to give.

COME FROM ON HIGH, MY KING AND GOD

Come from on high, my King and God,
  My Confidence thou art;
Display the Virtue of thy Blood,
  And circumcise my Heart.

From Heav'n, thy Holy Place, on me
  Descend in Mercy down;
Balm of the World, I thirst for Thee,
  To know Thee for my own.

From Top to Bottom rend the Veil
  That keeps me out of God;
Remove the Bar, and let me feel
  That I am thine Abode.

O might this worthless Heart of mine
  The Saviour's Temple be!
Empty'd of ev'ry Love but Thine,
  And shut to all but Thee!

I long to find thy Presence there,
  I long to see thy Face;
Almighty Lord, my Heart Prepare
  The Saviour to embrace.

Thou know'st, O Lord, no Rest I have
  By Reason of my Sin;
Convince me of thy Pow'r to save,
  And Say, "I will, be Clean."

I KNOW THAT IN MY FLESH DWELLETH NO GOOD THING

LORD, is not all from Thee?
Is not all Fullness Thine?
Whate'er of Good there is in me,
O Lord, is none of Mine.

Each Holy Tendency
Did not thy Mercy give?
And what, O Saviour, what have I
That I did not receive?

I cannot speak a Word
Or think a Thought that's Good,
But what proceedeth from the Lord,
And cometh forth from GOD.

JESUS, I know full well
What my best Actions be;
They'd sink my guilty Soul to Hell,
If unrefin'd by Thee.

Myself and all I do
O sprinkle with thy Blood;
Renew me, Saviour, e're I go
To stand before my GOD.

I, of myself, have nought
That can his Justice please;
Not one right word, nor Act, nor Thought
But what I owe to Grace.

O make my guilty Heart
Completely pure within;

Author of Holiness thou art,
And Finisher of Sin:

Cut short it's Reign in me,
Who only can'st subdue;
And give me all thy Grace to see,
Created *here* anew.

WHOM HAVE I IN HEAVEN

Whom have I in heaven but thee? and there is none upon earth that I desire beside thee.—Psalm 73:25.

Whom have I in Heav'n but Thee
Who bought'st my Soul with Blood?
What is all the Earth to me
If I am out of God?
Still my Woes are unredrest
If thou my Saviour wilt not be;
All is Vanity but Christ,
And worse than Vanity.

If my Lord Himself reveal,
No other Good I want;
Only Christ my Wounds can heal
Or silence my Complaint:
He that suffer'd in my stead,
The Lamb, shall my Physician be;
I will not be comforted
'Till Jesus comforts me.

All is Bitterness 'till then,
'Till I, through Grace, am thine;
'Till thy Sp'rit hath made me clean,
And seal'd thy Merits mine;
'Till my Ethiop Soul becomes
Partaker of thy Purity,
Sin to endless Exile dooms,
And thou art form'd in me.

Saviour, what retards thy Love,
That thou no nearer art?
Ev'ry Stumbling-block remove
That keeps Thee from my Heart;

Come, Redeemer, to my Breast,
As a refining Flame appear:
Be my Soul's eternal Guest,
And live and govern there.

Let the Mind that was in Thee
My Heart throughout renew;
Thou the only Model be
Of all I think or do:
Let me look to CHRIST alone
Who dy'd his Creature to redeem;
Build on this Foundation Stone,
And stand complete in Him.

PART II.

Mediator, intercede,
And I shall be forgiv'n;
Only for thy Judas plead,
And I am sure of Heav'n:
Thou my Substitute wast made;
My Sins, my Fears, my Misery,
All, Redeemer, all were laid,
With amplest Weight, on Thee.

Ev'ry idle Word I spoke
Or shall hereafter speak,
Made it still an heavier Yoke
That prest thy sacred Neck:
Yet my gracious Saviour stands
To give me Heav'n and Peace again,
Whom my Sin, with wicked Hands,
Hath crucify'd and slain.

At IMMANUEL's swift Approach
The Pow'rs of Hell shall fly;
Lord, at thy all-conqu'ring Touch
The Man of Sin shall die:
Touch me, LORD, thou seest how black,
How leprous, how defil'd I am;
Let me hear the Saviour speak
The Wonders of his Name.

When my LORD hath made me clean,
The carnal Mind is o'er;
Satan, Self, the World and Sin
Shall never conquer more:
I shall lead them all in Chains
If He the Strength of Faith impart;
Not a Spot of Sin remains
When CHRIST is in the Heart.

REFUGE IN THE RIGHTEOUSNESS OF CHRIST

From thy supreme Tribunal, LORD,
  Where Justice sits severe,
I to thy Mercy Seat appeal,
  And beg Forgiveness there.

Tho' I have sinn'd, before the Throne
  My Advocate I see:
JESUS, be thou my Judge, and let
  My Sentence come from Thee.

Lo, weary to thy Cross I fly
  There let me Shelter find:
LORD, when thou call'st thy ransom'd Home,
  O leave not me behind!

I joyfully embrace thy Love
  To fallen Man reveal'd;
My Hope of Glory, dearest LORD,
  On Thee alone I build.

The Law was satisfy'd by Him
  Who Flesh for me was made:
It's *Penalty* he underwent,
  It's *Precepts* he obey'd.

Desert and all Self-Righteousness
  I utterly forego;
My Robe of everlasting Bliss,
  My Wedding Garment *Thou!*

The spotless Saviour *liv'd* for me,
  And *dy'd* upon the Mount:
Th' Obedience of his Life and Death
  Is plac'd to my Account.

Can'st thou forget that awful Hour,
That sad, tremendous Scene,
When thy dear Blood on *Calvary*
Flow'd out at ev'ry Vein?

No, Saviour, no; thy Wounds are fresh,
Ev'n *now* they intercede;
Still, *in effect*, for guilty Man
Incessantly they bleed.

Thine Ears of Mercy still attend
A contrite Sinner's Cries,
A broken Heart that groans for God
Thou never wilt despise.

O Love incomprehensible
That made Thee bleed for me!
The Judge of all hath suffer'd Death
To set his Pris'ner free!

BENEATH THY COOL, REFRESHING SHADE

Beneath thy cool, refreshing Shade
  My Soul shall safely rest,
Jesus shall make my Spirit glad,
  And God shall be my Guest.

O may he all my Heart possess,
  And may I, when made clean,
The Self-denying Footsteps trace
  Of Him who did no Sin!

Gard'ner of Souls, thy Vineyard dress,
  Pluck up the Tares, O God:
And leave no Root of Bitterness,
  No Passion unsubdu'd.

Let nothing alienate the Soul
  For which the Saviour bled:
No Bosom Sin my Heart controul,
  Or choke the heav'nly Seed.

Far, far away the World be driv'n,
  And crucify'd to me;
May I in Heart ascend to Heav'n,
  And hourly learn of Thee!

Attack'd by Satan's fell Deceit,
  May I remain unshook,
And, piercing through the gilded Bait,
  Descry the deep-laid Hook.

FOR PARDON OF SIN

O might my Groans as Incense rise,
A fragrant, welcome Sacrifice,
  A Tribute freely giv'n!
Permit me to unfold my Care,
And, by th' Omnipotence of Pray'r,
  To scale the Walls of Heav'n!

But, Lord, how can I ask aright,
Depriv'd of thine assisting Light,
  And void of Grace within?
Full well I know my own Desert,
And tremble, lest my faithless Heart
  Should turn my Pray'r to Sin.

Unwash'd, unsprinkled with thy Blood,
O may I hear the Voice of God,
  And thy Salvation see!
Bid me look up with Faith at last,
And all the Depths of Mercy taste
  That lie conceal'd in Thee.

Jesus, thy Feet I will not leave,
'Till I the precious Gift receive,
  The purchas'd Pearl possess:
Impart it, gracious Lord, while I
With Supplication's humblest Cry
  Invest the Throne of Grace.

Baptize me with the Holy Ghost;
Make this the Day of Pentecost,
  Wherein my Soul may prove
Thy Spirit's sweet renewing Pow'r,

And shew me, in this happy Hour,
The Riches of thy Love.

Thou can'st not *always* hide thy Face,
Thou wilt at last my Soul embrace,
Thou yet wilt make me clean:
My God, is there not Room for me?
I'll wait with Patience, Lord, on Thee,
'Till thou shalt take me in!

PART II.

Remember, Lord, that Jesus bled,
That Jesus bow'd his dying Head
And sweated bloody Sweat:
He bore thy Wrath and Curse for me
In his own Body on the Tree,
And more than paid my Debt.

Surely he hath my Pardon bought,
A perfect Righteousness wrought out
His People to Redeem:
O that his Righteousness might be
By Grace imputed now to *me,*
As were my Sins to *Him!*

Saviour, thy Mercies cannot fail,
The Fund is inexhaustible,
For Thou wert pierc'd for me:
Then let me grasp the glorious Prize
Before me, and this Moment rise
A perfect Man in Thee.

THOU SUN OF RIGHTEOUSNESS ARISE

Thou Sun of Righteousness arise,
Shine, glorious Morning Star,
Enlighten my benighted Soul,
And make the Ethiop fair.

Confus'd and blind tho' now I am,
And prone to go astray,
Bid me receive my Sight, and I
Shall clearly see my Way.

The Captive, at thy Word, shall be
From ev'ry Chain releas'd;
The broken Heart, shall sing for Joy,
The troubled Sea shall rest.

Enflame me with a Ray of Heav'n,
Pure, fervent Love inspire;
And let thy dovelike Spirit aid
And fan the holy Fire.

Be thou my Light, for Light Thou art,
O crucify each Doubt;
Sweep ev'ry Corner of my Heart,
And turn the Tempter out.

Let not my Hopes be over-cast
With Shadows of Despair;
Dart through my Soul thy quick'ning Beams,
And build an Altar there.

Redeem me from Temptation's Rage,
Break down the Holds of Sin;
Give me to stand in crooked Ways,
And keep my Garments clean.

Transplant me, Saviour, from myself,
  And graft me into Thee;
Then shall the Grain of Mustard-seed
  Spring up into a Tree.

LET THIS MIND BE IN YOU WHICH WAS ALSO IN CHRIST JESUS

(Philippians 2:5)

Lord, I feel a carnal Mind
  That hangs about me still,
Vainly tho' I strive to bind
  My own rebellious Will;
Is not Haughtiness of Heart
  The Gulph between my God and me?
Meek Redeemer, now impart
  Thine own Humility.

Fain would I my Lord pursue,
  Be all my Saviour taught,
Do as Jesus bid me do,
  And think as Jesus thought:
But 'tis Thou must change my Heart,
  The perfect Gift must come from Thee:
Meek Redeemer, now impart
  Thine own Humility.

Lord, I cannot, must not rest
  'Till I thy Mind obtain,
Chase Presumption from my Breast
  And all thy Mildness gain;
Give me, Lord, thy gentle Heart,
  Thy lowly Mind my Portion be:
Meek Redeemer, now impart
  Thine own Humility.

Let thy Cross my Will control;
  Conform me to my Guide;
In the Manger lay my Soul,
  And crucify my Pride;

Give me, Lord, a contrite Heart,
An Heart that always looks to Thee:
Meek Redeemer, now impart
Thine own Humility.

Tear away my ev'ry Boast,
My stubborn Mind abase;
Saviour, fix my only Trust
In thy redeeming Grace:
Give me a submissive Heart,
From Pride and Self-dependance free;
Meek Redeemer, now impart
Thine own Humility!

FOR ALL THE MIND OF CHRIST

Hail, faultless Model, Sinless Guide,
In whom no Blame was seen!
Able Thou wert, and none beside,
To ransom guilty Men.

I want my Happiness below
In Thee alone to find;
Surely Thou wilt on me bestow
Thy *pure*, thy *heavenly* Mind!

Active for God I fain would be,
And do my Work assign'd:
Jesus, look down, implant in me
Thy *zealous, fervent* Mind!

While here, it was thy constant Aim
To benefit Mankind:
O give me, dear redeeming Lamb,
Thy *loving, gracious* Mind!

Stiff is my Neck and proud my Heart,
Unbroken, unresign'd;
When wilt thou, blessed Lord, impart
Thy *patient, humble* Mind!

My Sins how slowly do I leave,
To earthly Things inclin'd!
But wean me, Lord, and let me have
Thy *Self-denying* Mind!

O might I walk with faithful Heed,
And look no more behind,
Possest of what I chiefly need,
Thy *serious, steady* Mind!

Still may my ev'ry Grace increase,
'Till I in Heav'n appear:
On Earth like Thee in *Holiness,*
Like Thee in *Glory* There.

FOR PARDON

Now, LORD, the purchas'd Pardon give,
Nor e'er the Grant revoke,
But bend my stiff, obdurate Neck
Beneath thine easy Yoke.

O might I, as a faithful Sheep,
My Shepherd ne'er forsake!
O might I now for Heav'n set out,
And never more turn back!

CHRIST in his Resurrection's Pow'r
Within my Heart reveal:
Forgive my deep Revoltings, LORD,
And my Forgiveness *seal.*

Thou only hast the Words of Life,
My Soul to Thee-ward draw:
Me to thy Kingdom, LORD, instruct,
And teach me in thy Law.

Apollos waters but in vain,
Paul plants without Success;
The Prophet's Labours fruitless are
Except thou give Increase.

The great Increase thou wilt send down,
For thou hast shed thy Blood:
I shall thy Faithfulness proclaim
When I am born of GOD.

SHOULDEST THOU BE STRICT TO MARK OUR FAULTS

Shouldest thou be strict to mark our Faults,
Who could acquitted be?
Who, unrenew'd, could stand the Search,
Or bear the Scrutiny?

Lord, at thy Feet I meekly fall,
Held in Contrition's Chain:
Thy gracious Hand that cast me down
Shall raise me up again.

O speak the Word, thy Servant hears,
Pronounce me pardon'd now:
Lord, I believe, increase my Faith,
And let me know Thee too.

Thou only, Saviour, hast the Key,
Unlock the Prison Door!
Tho' yet I cannot fly to Thee,
I'll send my Heart before.

The Blood of sprink'ling now apply,
And that shall make me clean;
Weigh not my drossy Merits, Lord,
But O forgive my Sin.

Take now away whate'er obstructs
Thine Intercourse with me:
And may I, in Return, leave all
I have to follow Thee!

JESUS, THY POWER I FAIN WOULD FEEL

JESUS, thy Pow'r I fain wou'd feel,
Thy Love is all I want:
O let thine Ears consider well
The Voice of my Complaint.

Thou see'st me yet a Slave to Sin,
And destitute of GOD;
O purify and make me clean
By thine All-cleansing Blood.

Far off I stand, O bring me nigh,
And bid me sit up high'r:
IMMANUEL, now in Love pass by,
And answer my Desire.

O JESUS, undertake for me,
Thy Peace to me be giv'n:
For while I stand away from Thee
I stand away from Heav'n.

I will not my Offence conceal,
I will not hide my Sin,
But all my Crimes with Weeping tell,
And own how vile I've been.

LORD, will thy wrathful Jealousy
As Fire for ever burn?
And wilt Thou not a Succour be,
And Comfort those that Mourn?

Reject not, LORD, my humble Pray'rs,
Nor yet my Soul destroy:
Thine only Son hath sown in Tears
That I might reap in Joy.

HYMNS OF PRAISE
(EUCHARISTIC HYMNS)

"Immensa Beneficia Laudibus immensis celebranda."
PRIMAS.

O Thou Patron-God,
Thou God and Mortal, thence more *God to Man,*
Man's Theme eternal, Man's eternal Theme!
Thou canst not 'scape uninjured *from our Praise.*
NIGHT THOUGHTS. NT. 9.

PRAISE FOR CONVERSION

Not to myself I owe
That I, O Lord, am Thine;
Free Grace hath all the Shades broke through,
And caus'd the Light to shine

Me thou hast willing made
Thy offers to receive;
Call'd by the Voice that wakes the Dead,
I come to Thee and live.

Why am I made to see
Who am by nature blind?
Why am I taken home to Thee,
And others left behind?

Because thy sov'reign Love
Was bent the Worst to save:
Jesus, who reigns inthron'd above,
The free Salvation gave.

Tho' once far off I stood,
Nor knew myself thy Foe,
Brought nigh by the Redeemer's Blood,
Myself and Thee I know:

No more a Child of Wrath,
Thy Graciousness I see;
And praise thee for the Work of Faith
Which Thou hast wrought in me.

In Sins and Trespasses
When more than dead I lay,
Drew near my Tomb the Prince of Peace,
And roll'd the Stone away:

With me his Spirit strove,
Almighty to retrieve;
He saw me in a Time of Love,
And said unto me, Live.

By Him made free indeed,
I *felt* his gracious Words;
His Mantle over me was spread,
And I became the LORD's.

JESUS, thy Son, by Grace,
I to the End shall be;
Made perfect through thy Comeliness
Which I receiv'd from Thee.

I drink the living Stream
To all Believers giv'n,
A Fellow-citizen with Them
Who dwell in yonder Heav'n:

With all thy chosen Band
I trust to see Thee there,
And, in thy Righteousness, to stand
Undaunted at thy Bar.

THE HEAVENS DECLARE THE GLORY OF GOD

The Sky's a Veil, the outward Scene
Proclaims the Majesty within;
Which boundless Light, tho' hid behind,
Breaks out, too great to be confin'd.

The Heav'n thy glorious Impress bears,
Thy Image glitters in the Stars:
The Firmament, thine high Abode,
Seems too the spangled Robe of God.

Whene'er it's Beauty I admire,
It's radiant Globes direct me high'r:
In silent Praise they point to Thee,
All Light, all Eye, all Majesty!

Glory to Him who studs the Sky
(Earth's variegated Canopy)
With Lamps to guide us on our Way,
Faint Emblems of eternal Day,

Yes, Lord, each shining Orb declares
Thy Name in dazzling Characters;
As precious Gems they dart their Rays,
And seem to form a Crown of Praise.

ON ASCENSION DAY

Lo! the God by whom Salvation
  Is to fallen Man restor'd,
Now resumes his blissful Station,
  Shews Himself th' Almighty Lord;
Slow ascending,
Bids us, for a while, farewell.

Who his heav'nly State suspended,
  And for Man's Atonement died,
By unnumber'd Hosts attended
  Rises to his Father's Side;
Born by Angels
Back to his eternal Throne.

Seraphs, chaunt his endless Praises,
  Guard Him to his ancient Seat;
Open wide, ye heav'nly Places,
  Your returning God admit:
Heav'nly Portals
Let the King of Glory in!

Christ his Kingdom re-inherits,
  His before the World began;
Myriads of admiring Spirits
  Hover round the Son of Man;
Wrapt in Wonder,
View the Wounds he bore for us.

"Worthy Thou of Exaltation,"
  Lost in sweet Surprize, they sing;
"Mortals, with like Acclamation,
  Hail your great redeeming King:
Let your Voices
Emulate th' angelic Choir."

Yes, O Christ, from ev'ry Creature
Praise shall to thy Name be giv'n;
Worthy Thou of more and greater,
King of Saints and King of Heav'n!
Kindling Transports
Swell our Hearts and tune our Tongues!

Tho' our Lord is taken from us,
Present but in Spirit now,
This his faithful Word of Promise
Made while Sojourning below;
"Where I enter
Thither shall my Servant come."

Him we praise for his Ascension,
Conqueror of Sin and Death;
Gone up to prepare a Mansion
For his ransom'd Flock beneath:
They shall quickly
Reign with Him in Glory there.

There already is our Treasure,
There our Heart, our Hope, our Crown;
Thence on sublunary Pleasure
We, with holy Scorn, look down:
Earth hath nothing
Worth a Moment's transient Thought.

We shall soon in Bliss adore Thee,
Gain the Realms of endless Day;
Soon be gathered Home to Glory,
All our Tears be wip'd away:
There, for ever,
Sing the Lamb's new Song of Love.

TO THE TRINITY

Glorious Union, God unsought,
Three in Name and one in Thought,
All thy Works thy Goodness show,
Center of Perfection Thou.

Praise we, with uplifted Eyes,
Him that dwells above the Skies:
God, who reigns on *Sion's* Hill,
Made, redeem'd, and *keeps* us still.

Join th' angelic Hosts above,
Praise the Father's matchless Love,
Who for us his Son hath giv'n,
Sent Him to regain our Heav'n.

Glory to the Saviour's Grace,
Help of *Adam's* helpless Race;
Who, for our Transgressions slain,
Makes us one with God again.

Next, the Holy Ghost we bless;
He *makes known* and *seals* our Peace:
Us he cleanses and makes whole,
Quickens ev'ry dying Soul.

Holy, blessed, glorious Three,
One from all Eternity,
Make us Vessels of thy Grace,
Ever running o'er with Praise.

Thee we laud with grateful Song,
Sever'd from the guilty Throng,
Ransom'd by the Son who died,
By the Spirit *sanctify'd.*

All the Persons join to raise
Sinners to a State of Grace;
All unite their Bliss t' insure,
In the glorious Work concur.

O that we his Love might taste!
Bless us, and we shall be blest;
Cleanse us, LORD, from Sin's Abuse,
Fit us for the Master's Use.

In our Hearts, thy Temples, dwell;
With the Hope of Glory fill:
Be on Earth *our* Guest divine,
Then let Heav'n make us *thine*.

FATHER, LORD OF ALL MANKIND

Father, LORD of all Mankind,
Thee we attempt to sing;
With thy Son and Spirit join'd,
Our everlasting King;
Us Thou dost in CHRIST receive,
Cloth'd with CHRIST we come to Thee:
Him thou did'st for Sinners give
Their *Substitute* to be.

All our Sins, O Lamb of GOD,
Are for thy Sake, forgiv'n;
JESUS', thy restoring Blood
Entitles Men to Heav'n:
Self-existent, LORD of All,
Uncreate, with GOD the same,
Bought by Thee on Thee we call,
Exulting in thy Name.

Spirit of Jehovah, write
Thy Nature on our Heart,
Us unto the LORD unite
As Thou united art;
Make us meet his Face to see,
JESUS' Righteousness apply:
Holy Ghost, our Leader be,
And guide us to the Sky.

Three in one, before thy Feet
Our inmost Souls we bend,
Glorious Mystery, too great
For Worms to comprehend:

We can ne'er, on this side Death,
Bring the Deity to Light;
Reason here must yield to Faith,
'Till Faith is lost in Sight.

JESUS, THOU TRIED FOUNDATION STONE

Jesus, thou tried Foundation Stone,
From whose prevailing Blood alone
  Thy Saints expect Salvation,
My Robe thou art, I feel thy Grace,
And triumph in thy Righteousness
  Made mine by Imputation.

Exulting in thy Strength I go,
My allotted Work rejoice to do,
  For Love divine constrains me:
Supported inwardly by This,
Through ev'ry obstacle I press
  While thy great Arm sustains me.

By thy free Grace 'till now upheld,
My future Hopes on Thee I build,
  Nor are my Hopes ill-grounded:
Thy Promises are on my Side,
And safe to Glory, lo! I ride,
  By countless Deaths surrounded.

Before I from the Body fly,
He who *forgave* shall *sanctify*
  And perfectly *renew* me;
Stronger than Satan JESUS is;
Sin shall not always wound my Peace,
  Nor finally subdue me.

Who wash'd me from it's deadly *Stain,*
Shall here cut short it's guilty *Reign,*
  And weaken it's *Dominion;*
From Height to Height my Faith shall rise,

Until I gain my native Skies
  On Love's seraphic Pinion.

Unmov'd, 'till then, on CHRIST I stand,
And Satan from the Saviour's Hand
  In vain attempts to stir me:
On JESUS I for Strength depend;
My omnipotent, redeeming Friend,
  Prepares my Way before me.

PRAISE THE LORD MY JOYFUL HEART

Praise the Lord, my joyful Heart,
With the Elders bear thy Part:
Stand with them around the Throne,
Singing Praises to the Son.

Strive with them, in Rapture lost,
Who shall laud the Saviour most:
Join with Angels to proclaim
All the Mercies of the Lamb.

Praise his great Humility
Long as Life remains in Thee:
By thy Pray'rs and Praises giv'n
Make on Earth a Demi-heav'n.

Jesus, I the Theme renew
Endless Praises are thy Due:
Anthems equal to thy Grace
Saints and Angels cannot raise.

I my worthless Mite cast in,
Here the Song of Heav'n begin:
I th' eternal Chorus join,
Echoing the Love divine.

Ever may I worship Thee,
Praise my sole Employment be;
Ev'ry Moment thank my God,
Sing the Virtues of thy Blood!

MY SOUL WITH BLESSINGS UNCONFINED

My Soul with Blessings unconfin'd
  Thy tender Care supplies;
Thyself the Fountain Head from whence
  Those Blessings first arise.

May I thy gracious Gifts receive
  With Gratitude and Joy,
And in thy just, deserved Praise
  Each thankful Hour employ.

And may thy condescending Love
  That Gratitude receive,
Which, tho' a trifling Sacrifice,
  Is all a Worm can give!

THE WITNESS OF THE SPIRIT

The Spirit itself beareth witness with our Spirit, that we are the Children of God.—ROMANS 8:16.

Earnest of future Bliss,
  Thee, Holy Ghost, we hail;
Fountain of Holiness
  Whose Comforts never fail.
The cleansing Gift on Saint's bestow'd,
The Witness of their Peace with GOD.

With our Perverseness here
  How often hast thou strove,
And spar'd us Year by Year
  With never-ceasing Love!
O set from Sin our Spirits free,
And make us more and more like Thee.

What wondrous Grace is this
  For GOD to dwell with Men!
Through JESUS' Righteousness
  His Favour we regain,
And feeble Worms, by Nature lost,
Are Temples of the Holy Ghost.

Tho' *Belial's* Sons would prove
  That thou *no* Witness art,
Thanks to redeeming Love,
  We feel Thee in our Heart;
O may'st thou still persist to bear
Thine inward Testimony there.

By Thee on Earth we know
  Ourselves in CHRIST renew'd,
Brought by thy Grace into
  The Family of God:

Of his adopting Love the Seal,
And faithful Teacher of his Will.

Great Comforter, descend,
  In gentle Breathings down;
Preserve us to the End,
  That no Man take our Crown:
Our Guardian still vouchsafe to be
Nor suffer us to go from Thee.

THANKSGIVING FOR THE DIVINE FAITHFULNESS

Immoveable our Hope remains,
Within the Veil our Anchor lies;
JESUS, who wash'd us from our Stains,
Shall bear us safely to the Skies.

Strong in his Strength, we boldly say,
For us IMMANUEL shed his blood;
Who then shall tear our Shield away,
Or part us from the Love of GOD?

Can Tribulation or Distress,
Or Persecution's fiery Sword?
Can Satan rob us of our Peace,
Or prove too mighty for the LORD?

Founded on CHRIST, secure we stand,
Seal'd with his Spirit's inward Seal;
We soon shall gain the promis'd Land,
Triumphant o'er the powers of Hell.

The Winds may roar, the Floods may beat;
And Rain, impetuous, descend;
Yet will he not his own forget,
But love and save them to the End.

JESUS acquits, and who condemns?
Cease, Satan, from thy fruitless Strife:
Thy Malice cannot reach our Names
To blot them from the Book of Life.

This is eternal Life to know
GOD and the Lamb for Sinners giv'n:
Nor will the Saviour let us go,
His ransom'd Candidates for Heav'n.

Us to redeem his Life he paid,
And will He not his Purchase have?
Who can behold IMMANUEL bleed,
And doubt his Willingness to save?

Surely the Son hath made us free,
Who Earth, and Heav'n and Hell commands;
Our Cause of Triumph this—that we
Are graven on the Saviour's Hands.

To Him who wash'd us in his Blood,
And lifts apostate Man to Heav'n,
And reconciles his Sheep to GOD,
Be everlasting Glory giv'n.

ON THE BIRTH OF CHRIST

Amplest Grace in Thee I find,
Friend and Saviour of Mankind,
Richest Merit to atone
For our Sins before the Throne.

Born to save a World from Hell,
Once thou did'st with Sinners dwell;
Wert to Earth a Prophet giv'n,
Now our Advocate in Heav'n.

Well might wond'ring Angels cry,
"Glory be to God on high,
Peace on Earth, good Will to Men,
Lost Mankind is found again."

Join, my Soul, their holy Song,
Emulate the brighter Throng,
Hail the everlasting Word,
Welcome thy descending Lord.

Grace unequal'd! Love unknown!
Jesus lays aside his Crown,
Cloaths Himself with Flesh and Blood,
Takes the Manhood into God.

Harden'd Rebels though we are,
Lo! He comes to sojourn here:
See Him lie where Oxen feed;
This his Chamber, Hay his Bed!

God (O hear it with Surprize!)
For a Manger leaves the Skies,
By assuming Flesh beneath,
Render'd capable of Death.

From their Maker turn'd aside,
As in *Adam* all have died,
So whoe'er his Grace receive,
Shall in Christ be made alive.

THANKSGIVING FOR GENERAL MERCIES

Gracious Creator, thy kind Hand
  In all thy Works I see:
Resistless Pow'r and mildest Love
  Are blended, LORD, in Thee.

When Thou art wroth and hid'st thy Face,
  The whole Creation mourns,
For thou'rt th' attractive Pole to which
  The World's great Needle turns.

O let my Heart be wholly thine,
  Thy Property alone!
No longer let me think it mine,
  Or call myself my own!

Without Reserve I quit the Claim
  And give up all to Thee,
For thou, my All-sufficient LORD,
  Art more than all to me.

Only do thou refine my Dross,
  And cleanse me with thy Blood,
To make th' imperfect Sacrifice
  Acceptable to GOD.

Nor shall I fear, if JESUS pleads,
  Unworthy as I am,
Being excluded from the Feast
  And Supper of the Lamb.

THANKSGIVING FOR THE RIGHTEOUSNESS OF CHRIST

Fountain of never-ceasing Grace,
Thy Saint's exhaustless Theme,
Great Object of immortal Praise,
Essentially supreme;
We bless Thee for the glorious Fruits
Thy Incarnation gives,
Thy Righteousness which Grace *imputes*,
And Faith alone *receives*.

Whom Heav'n's angelic Host adores,
Was slaughter'd for our Sin;
The *Guilt*, O Lord, was wholly ours,
The *Punishment* was thine:
Our God in Flesh, to set us free,
Was manifested here;
And meekly bore our Sins, that we
His Righteousness might wear.

Imputatively guilty then
Our Substitute was made,
That we the Blessings might obtain
For which his Blood was shed:
Himself he offer'd on the Cross
Our Sorrows to remove;
And all he *suffer'd* was for us,
And all he *did* was Love.

In Him we have a Righteousness
By God Himself approv'd;
Our Rock, our sure Foundation this,
Which never can be mov'd:
Our Ransom by his Death he paid,

For all his People giv'n,
The Law he perfectly obey'd.
That they might enter Heav'n.

As All, when *Adam*, sinn'd alone,
In his Transgression died,
So by the Righteousness of one
Are Sinners justify'd:
We to thy Merit, precious LORD,
With humblest joy, submit;
Again to Paradise restor'd,
In *Thee* alone complete.

Our Souls his watchful Love retrieves,
Nor lets them go astray;
His Righteousness to us he gives,
And takes our Sins away.
We claim Salvation in his Right,
Adopted and forgiv'n;
His Merit is our Robe of Light,
His Death the Gate of Heav'n.

THANKSGIVING FOR THE SUFFERINGS OF CHRIST

O thou who did'st thy Glory leave
Apostate Sinners to retrieve
From Nature's deadly Fall,
Me thou hast purchas'd with a Price,
Nor shall my Crimes in Judgment rise,
For Thou hast born Them all.

JESUS was punish'd in my stead,
Without the Gate my Surety bled
To expiate my Stain:
On Earth the *Godhead* deign'd to dwell,
And made of infinite Avail
The Suff'rings of the *Man*.

And was he for his Rebels giv'n?
He was: Th' incarnate King of Heav'n
Did for his Foes expire:
Amaz'd, O Earth, the Tidings hear;
He bore, that we might never bear,
His Father's righteous Ire.

Ye Saints, the Man of Sorrows bless,
The GOD for your Unrighteousness
Deputed to atone:
Praise Him, 'till, with the heav'nly Throng,
Ye sing the Never-ending Song,
And see Him on his Throne.

THE GENERAL THANKSGIVING IN THE LITURGY

(Paraphrased)

Eternal God, the Thanks receive
Which thine unworthy Servants give;
Father of ev'ry Mercy Thou,
Almighty and all-gracious too!

In humble, yet exulting Songs,
Thy Praises issue from our Tongues,
For that incessant, boundless Love
Which we and all thy Creatures prove.

Fashion'd by thy creating Hand,
And by thy Providence sustain'd,
We fain our Gratitude would shew
For all thy *temp'ral* Blessings due.

But O! for THIS we chiefly raise
Our Anthems of immortal Praise—
For Thine inestimable Love
Which sent IMMANUEL from above.

For HIM, of all thy Gifts the best,
Th' *exceeding* Gift that crowns the rest,
For HIM thy gracious Name we laud,
And bless Thee for a Suff'ring God.

Nor should we fail our Lord to praise,
For all th' assisting Means of Grace;
Th' appointed Channels which convey
Strength to support us on our Way.

To Thee let all our Thanks be giv'n
For our well-grounded Hope of Heav'n;
Our glorious Trust that we shall reign
And live with Him who died for Man.

And O! so deep a Sense impress
Of thy supreme, unbounded Grace,
That Gratitude unfeign'd may rise,
And shake the Earth and pierce the Skies!

May we in Deed, as well as Word,
Shew forth the Praises of the LORD,
And thank Him still for what he gives
Both with our *Lips*, and in our *Lives!*

O that, by Sin no more subdu'd,
We might devote ourselves to GOD,
And only breathe to tell his Praise,
And in his Service spend our days!

Hail, Father! Hail, Co-equal Son!
Hail, sacred Spirit, Three in One!
Glory and Thanks and Pow'r Divine,
Thrice Holy LORD, be ever Thine!

SELECT PARAPHRASES

Sanctos ausus recludere Fontes.

PSALM 148

General Praise to God be giv'n;
Praise Him in the Height of Heav'n:
Him, ye glorious Hosts, proclaim,
Saints and Angels, bless his Name!

Sun, his lofty Praise display,
His who made thee King of Day:
Moon, adore the God of Light,
God, who made thee Queen of Night.

Stars, your Tribute, too, be giv'n,
Spangles in the Robe of Heav'n:
God, your awful Sov'reign, own,
Bright Successors of the Moon.

Praise, thou Curtain of the Sky,
(Hiding Heav'n from mortal Eye)
Him that spreads thy wat'ery Clouds;
Celebrate the God of Gods.

Highest Heav'n, his dwelling Place,
Lift thy Voice, resound his Praise:
Hymn "The Dweller ev'ry where."
Present more supremely there.

Sun, and Moon, and Stars, and Light,
Heav'n and Sky, and Clouds unite;
Verbal Creatures of the Lord,
Swift existing at his Word.

'Stablish'd firm by his Command,
Lo! immoveable ye stand;
Him, th' ineffable, adore,
Own his regulating Pow'r.

Womb and Sepulchre of Man,
Join, O Earth, the grateful Train;
Praise, 'till in the last great Fire,
Thou and all thy Works expire.

Ocean, with thy num'rous Brood,
Swell to magnify thy God:
Roll his Praise from Shore to Shore,
Lift his Name and sound his Pow'r.

Praise Him, Fire and Hail and Snow;
Praise Him all ye Winds that blow:
Cold and Heat—Let each extreme
Join to render Praise to Him.

PART II.

Storms dispensing Waste and Death,
Dreadful Messengers of Wrath;
Spread his Fear and Praise abroad,
Weapons of an angry God.

Mountains, Vales, and Hills, and Trees,
Tell how good your Maker is:
His exalted Praise declare,
Feather'd Songsters of the Air.

Beasts of Prey where'er ye prowl,
Join to make the Concert full:
Cattle, low Jehovah's Fame;
Meanest Insects, do the same.

Kings and People, Rich and Poor,
Celebrate creating Pow'r;
Made and ransom'd by the Lamb,
All extol the great I AM.

Female, Male, of ev'ry Age,
From the Suckling to the Sage,
All conspire with one accord,
Chaunt the Glories of the Lord.

Worthy Praise can ne'er be giv'n
'Till his Saints arrive at Heav'n,
There, with all the glorious ones,
Sing his Praise and cast their Crowns.

HE HATH BORN OUR GRIEFS[1]

Surely he hath borne our griefs, and carried our sorrows: yet we did esteem him stricken, smitten of God, and afflicted.
—Isaiah 53:4; also 53:5, 12.

Surely Christ thy Griefs hath borne;
Weeping Soul, no longer mourn:
View Him bleeding on the Tree,
Pouring out his Life for thee:
There thy ev'ry Sin he bore:
Weeping Souls, lament no more.

All thy Crimes on Him were laid:
See, upon his blameless Head
Wrath its utmost Vengeance pours,
Due to my Offence and yours:
Wounded in our Stead, He is;
Bruis'd for our Iniquities.

Weary Sinner, keep thine Eyes
On th' atoning Sacrifice:
There th' Incarnate Deity
Number' d with Transgressors see;
There his Father's Absence mourns;
Nail'd, and Bruis'd, and crown'd with Thorns.

See thy God his Head bow down;
Hear the Man of Sorrows groan;
For thy Ransom, there condemn'd;
Stript, derided, and blasphem'd:
Bleeds the guiltless for th' unclean:
Made an off'ring for thy Sin.

Cast thy guilty Soul on Him;
Find Him mighty to redeem;

1 This hymn was revised in after years; we give the latter version.

At his Feet thy Burden lay;
Look thy Doubts and Cares away:
Now, by Faith, the Son embrace;
Plead his Promise; trust his Grace.

Lord, thy Arm must be reveal'd,
Ere I can by Faith be heal'd;
Since I scarce can look to Thee,
Cast a gracious Eye on me!
At thy Feet myself I lay:
Shine, O shine my Fears away!

THE 12TH CHAPTER OF ISAIAH[1]

When thou, O Sinner art
  Created new in Heart,
Thou shalt feelingly proclaim
  What thy Lord hath done for thee;
Sav'd by his redeeming Name,
  Freed from Sin's Captivity.

Then shalt thou gladly say,
  In that triumphant Day,
Thee, my Saviour, will I praise,
  Praise thee even for thy Rod:
Me thou did'st afflict in Grace;
  Scourge, to bring me Home to God.

My Soul thou dost retrieve,
  And all my Sin forgive:
Thou did'st for a Season frown;
  (So it then appear'd to me);
But thy seeming Wrath is gone;
  I can now rejoice in thee.

My cause of Gladness, this:
  "God my Salvation is":
He, who did my Soul redeem,
  Gives me Confidence for Dread:
Chosen and secure in Him,
  I will scorn to be afraid.

Strength I from him derive;
  I on his Fulness live:
Never let my joyful Tongue
  Cease his Kindness to record!

1 This hymn was revised in after years; we give the latter version.

Thou, O Jesus, art my Song;
Thou my Prophet, Priest, and Lord.

Each Mourner too shall taste
Of this sublime Repast:
Jesus will their Fears destroy;
In their Hearts his Grace reveal:
They that weep shall draw, with Joy,
Water from Salvation's Well.

Fear not, thou waiting Soul;
Thy Joy shall soon be full:
Thou shalt of his Glory sing;
Tell his wond'rous Love abroad:
Thee he shall to Zion bring,
Sav'd by his availing Blood.

His Smile shall make thee know
An inward Heav'n below:
Thou, whom Man despises, shout;
Christ, whom thou dost wait to see,
Will in now wise cast thee out:
He shall dwell and walk in thee.

NAMES OF CHRIST—EXPRESSIVE OF HIS OFFICES

(Taken from various parts of Scripture)

Low at thy Feet, O Christ, we fall,
Enabled to confess,
And call thee by the Holy Ghost,
The *Lord our Righteousness.*

GOD over all IMMANUEL reigns,
With his great Father one;
The *Brightness of his Glory* thou,
And Partner of his Throne.

Author and *Finisher of Faith*
In all that know thy Name;
A furious *Lion* to thy Foes,
But to thy Friends a *Lamb:*

Sceptre of Israel, Prince of Peace:
Immortal *King of Kings:*
The *Sun of Righteousness* that shines
With Healing in his Wings:

The *Gift of God* to fallen Man:
The *Lord of Quick and Dead:*
A *Well of Life* to fainting Souls,
And their sustaining *Bread:*

Foundation of thy People's Joy,
Their Pardon and their Rest:
On Earth our *Sacrifice* for Sin,
In Heav'n our great *high Priest:*

The *Lord of Life*, who suffer'dst Death
That we might Heav'n regain:
The source of Blessing, who, on Earth,
Wert made a Curse for Man:

Wert poor that Adam's needy Sons
  Treasure in Thee might find:
Repairer of the dreadful Breach,
  Restorer of Mankind:

Through thy Desert, a fallen World
  To God may gain Access;
With thy fine Linen deck our Souls,
  Thy perfect Righteousness:

With that celestial Robe endu'd,
  We ev'ry Foe defy;
On Earth it shall our Armour be,
  Our Glory in the Sky.

THE PRAYER OF KING MANASSES

(Paraphrased)

Author of all in Earth and Sky,
From whom the Stars derive their Light;
When thou art wroth, the Planets die,
And melt as nothing in thy Sight:

Measur'd by thine almighty Hand,
Unfathom'd Seas of liquid Glass,
Obedient, owe thy high Command,
And keep the Bounds they cannot pass;

Shut up by their restraining LORD,
They in their proper Channels flow:
Obey JEHOVAH's sov'reign Word,
"Here, and no farther, shall ye go."

Thy Terrors, as a blazing Flame,
Devour and weigh the Sinner down:
The mighty tremble at thy Name,
And Nations quake beneath thy Frown.

Tremendous as thy Judgments are,
Thy Pity too no Limit knows:
Thine Arm is stretch'd the Meek to spare,
And terribly consume thy Foes.

With Shame, great GOD, I own with me
Thy ling'ring Mercy long hath borne,
Yet would I not come back to Thee,
Proudly refusing to return.

When Mercy call'd I stopt my Ear;
How did I from the Saviour rove,
And, bent on Death, refuse to hear
The Voice of thy inviting Love!

Blind were my Eyes, and Hard my Heart,
And proof against thy striving Grace;
I would from thee, my Strength, depart,
And cease to walk in Wisdom's Ways:

But Lo! on Thee I fix my Hope;
Be thou my Friend and Advocate;
Gracious Redeemer, lift me up,
And raise me to my first Estate.

Faith in thy Merit is thy Gift,
By which thou dost Backsliders heal:
Impart it, gracious LORD, to lift
My abject Soul from whence I fell.

PART II.

Repentance is not for the Just,
Whose Sin already is forgiv'n,
Whom thou hast rescu'd from the Lost,
And number'd with the Heirs of Heav'n:

To Sinners, of whom I am Chief,
Thy healing Promises pertain;
Who fell from Thee through Unbelief,
By Faith may be restor'd again.

Of treble Mercy I have need;
My Sins have took deep Hold on me:
In Number they the Grains exceed
That form the Margin of the Sea.

Meek on the Earth thy Servant lies,
And humbly makes his Sorrows known;
Unworthy to lift up my Eyes
To Heav'n, my injur'd Maker's Throne.

Bow'd with my Sense of Sin, I faint
Beneath the complicated Load;
Father, attend my deep Complaint,
I am thy Creature, thou my GOD!

Tho' I have broke thy righteous Law,
Yet with me let thy Spirit stay;
Nor from me utterly withdraw,
Nor take my Spark of Hope away.

Before thine awful Judgment Seat
My Heart's interior Knee I bow;
Survey my Sins with deep Regret;
But thou canst make them white as Snow.

Mercy unlimited is thine,
God of the Penitent thou art;
The saving Power of Blood divine
Shall wipe the Anguish from my Heart.

Then let not Sin my Ruin be,
Give me in thee my Rest to find:
JESUS, the Sick have Need of Thee,
The great Physician of Mankind.

In my Salvation, LORD, display
The Triumphs of abounding Grace:
Tell me my Guilt is done away,
And turn my Mourning into Praise.

Repriev'd so long from Hell's Abyss
Thou wilt not hurl me there at last,
But cheer me with the Smile of Peace,
Nor look at my Offences past.

Then shall I add my feeble Song
  To their's who chaunt thy Praise on high:
And spread, with an immortal Tongue,
  Thy Glory through the echoing Sky.

THE 20TH PSALM

Beloved of GOD, may JESUS hear
The ardent Breathings of thy Pray'r,
   And cancel thy Transgressions;
Be with thee in Affliction's Day,
Redeem thee from thy Fears, and say
   Amen to thy Petitions!

Thy every Need he will supply;
His Saints shall surely find him nigh,
   The GOD whom they rely on:
He will not turn away his Face,
But save thee from his Holy Place,
   And send thee Help from Sion.

Thy feeblest Pray'r shall reach his Throne;
Thy ev'ry Pang is noted down,
   And thou shalt be forgiven:
He loves thee, troubled as thou art;
And all the Pantings of thy Heart
   Are treasur'd up in Heaven.

GOD is our Triumph in Distress;
His Children's Privilege it is
   To smile at Tribulation:
JESUS, to Thee we lift our Voice,
By Grace enabled to rejoice
   In Hope of thy Salvation.

Ready to hear, O LORD, thou art,
Mighty to take thy People's Part
   And help them in Affliction:
Creation kneels to thy Command;

The Saving Strength of thy Right Hand
  Shall be our sure Protection.

In Chariots some repose their Trust,
Of Horses others make their Boast,
  But we in God are stronger:
Who on the Arm of Flesh rely,
Trembling before our Face shall fly,
  When we shall more than conquer.

Still may the Palm to us be giv'n;
Thy Saints, O mighty King of Heav'n,
  Continue to deliver:
Support us with thy strength'ning Grace,
'Till we, in yon celestial Place,
  Sit down with Thee for ever.

PSALM 119:169–176

Consider, LORD, my just Complaint;
Wisdom divine is what I want;
From Lack of Knowledge, LORD, I groan:
O when shall I my GOD put on?

O let my Supplication rise
As Fumes of Incense to the Skies,
Enter JEHOVAH's high Abode,
The Presence Chamber of my GOD!

When I am truly taught thy Ways
My Lips shall only speak thy Praise;
My Tongue shall sing of Thee alone,
And tell the Wonders thou hast done.

Assist me in thy Love to stand,
And hold me by thy guardian Hand;
Help me to choose the Lot of Grace,
The Way of Life, the Path of Peace.

LORD, I have long'd thy Will to know,
And, knowing, all thy Will to do:
My Meat and Drink is Thee to please,
And know the Saviour as he is.

Tho', as a Sheep, I went astray,
And wander'd from thy Holy Way,
(The Way that CHRIST, my Master trod,
The narrow Way that leads to GOD:)

Sought out by Grace, brought back I am,
Sav'd by the Merits of the Lamb:
And now, O CHRIST, myself I see,
In Adam lost, restor'd in Thee.

THE 121ST PSALM

My Heart, whene'er I lift my Eyes
  To Heaven's exalted Sphere,
Wing'd with impetuous Ardour, flies,
  To meet Thee in the Air.

JESUS by Faith I ever see,
  Who for the Sinner pleads,
And ev'ry Moment look to Thee,
  From whom my Help proceeds.

The great Artificer of Heav'n
  My Guard and Keeper is,
Who, by his Spirit inly giv'n,
  Assures me I am His.

Where'er I go he guides my Steps,
  Nor suffers me to fall:
Israel's Defence, who never sleeps,
  Surrounds me as a Wall.

In my Redeemer's watchful Sight
  Secure I ever stand;
My Guard by Day, my Screen by Night,
  My Shield on either Hand,

Knit to my condescending GOD,
  I dwell with the Supreme;
Nor open Force nor secret Fraud
  Shall sever me from Him.

His Light, his Peace, his Heav'n is mine,
  And mine his mighty Pow'r:
My faithful Sentinel-divine
  Preserves me ev'ry Hour.

My going out and coming in
He prospers with Success;
And while I keep myself from Sin,
He'll never love me less.

THE 134TH PSALM

Ye Friends and Followers of GOD,
With Robes made white in JESUS' Blood,
   Approach the Throne of Grace:
His Temple's hallow'd Court draw nigh,
By Day and Night renew the Cry,
   And sound the Trump of Praise.

With Ardour lift your Hearts and Hands;
In yonder Heav'n IMMANUEL stands
   To offer up your Pray'rs:
From *Sion* He your Souls shall bless;
Builder of Heav'n and Earth he is,
   And dwells above the Stars.

THE 4TH CHAPTER OF AMOS

Ye Kine of *Bashan*, who devour
The Needy and oppress the Poor,
Who drown in Wine your banish'd Sense,
And drink the Spoil of Violence;

God by his Holiness hath sworn
(The awful God whose Law ye scorn)
Your Foes, whom more than Him ye dread,
Your destin'd Borders shall invade.

The Lord hath ratify'd your Doom;
Yourselves and your's he will consume:
Aliens his Instruments shall be
To scourge your vile Idolatry.

Your stately Buildings then shall fall;
His Vengeance shall destroy them all:
Your Palaces shall be a Prey,
And Stalls for Oxen in that Day.

Shall guilty Hands and wanton Eyes
Be lifted up in Sacrifice?
Cease to transgress, and then my Ear
Shall meet the Incense of your Pray'r.

In vain my Judgments are abroad,
Tokens of an offended God;
Nor Wrath nor Mercies can prevail,
Nor Love of Heav'n nor Fear of Hell.

I gave you, in your greatest Need,
Cleanness of Teeth, through want of Bread;
Each Face was pale, and weak each Knee,
Yet have ye not return'd to me.

Have I not marr'd the rip'ning Grain
With scorching Heat and want of Rain?
And frustrated your rising Hopes
By wither'd Trees and blasted Crops?

Your Water fail'd, your Wells were dry;
Your Thirst ye could not satisfy:
Your fainting Cities yet sinn'd on,
And drew my fiercer Judgments down.

Your Figs and Olive Trees I smote,
Your Vineyards I consum'd with Drought;
Mildew and Palmer-worms bereft,
The Earth of what the Drought had left.

Contagious Sickness next I sent:
(Infatuate *Egypt's* Punishment)
My Fury next in Blood I pour'd,
And gave your Children to the Sword.

Horses (the Ruin who can tell?)
Promiscuous with their Riders fell:
Caus'd by their Stench, th' infectious Air
Increas'd the Havock of the War.

Obdurate still, ye felt mine Ire
Reveal'd from Heav'n in Flames of Fire:
The blazing Ruin swept away
Men, Towns, and Cities, in a Day.

But ye my pitying Grace repriev'd,
As Firebrands from the Burning sav'd;
But O! repriev'd in vain! for still
Ye dare the fiercer Flames of Hell.

Hear then the Message of the LORD,
The awful Thunder of his Word;
Since all my Judgments strive in vain
To kindle Fear in stubborn Man,

Myself in Judgment shall appear,
And call thee, *Israel*, to my Bar:
As harden'd *Pharoah*, blind and proud,
Prepare to meet thy hostile GOD!

Prepare to meet your dreadful Foe,
Omniscient and Almighty too;
Whose Terrors Heav'n and Earth proclaim—
The GOD of Glory is his Name.

PSALM 119:9–17

Wherewith, O SAVIOUR, may
A young Man cleanse his Way?
How his rising Passions tame,
How be Holy as his LORD?
He his ev'ry Deed must frame
By the Model of thy Word.

Thou my Director be,
Conduct my Steps to Thee:
With my Heart I thee have sought;
LORD, in me thy Law reveal,
Guide me that I wander not,
Help me to perform thy Will.

I have laid up the Word
And Precept of my LORD
As a precious Pearl within;
That my secret Treasure is,
My Preservative from Sin:
All I want lies hid in this.

Happy my Soul shall be
When taught, O CHRIST, of thee:
Led by thee into all Truth,
With my lips I shall declare
All the Judgments of thy Mouth,
Tell Mankind how right they are.

Blest in the Saviour's Love,
My Treasure is above:
Sweetly of my GOD possest,
Rich in Him, I need no more;

Envy not the Miser's Chest,
Naked, mid'st his Heaps, and Poor.

My Talk shall ever be,
Jesus, concerning Thee:
Thee I'll Eye in all I do,
Ever look to thee my Lord,
Keep thy Statutes still in View,
Guided by the written Word.

PSALM 119:161–169

Princes have persecuted me,
But, Lord, my Trust is still in Thee;
Me from my Hope they sought to move,
But could not stir me from thy Love.

I fly for Refuge to my Lord,
For Comfort to his healing Word:
From *Saul* my safe Retreat he is,
And all the Troublers of my Peace.

Each passing Hour displays his Care;
He saves me from the latent Snare:
His Love with Wonder I survey,
And praise him seven Times a Day.

Jesus, my Mind from Earth withdraw;
Great Peace have they that love thy Law:
No Precept there which thou hast giv'n
Is hard to them who strive for Heav'n.

I too have look'd thy Health to see,
And taste the Peace that comes from thee;
Each inward Lust have strove to kill,
And walk in all thy perfect Will.

My Soul hath lov'd thy Ways and Thee:
The Law is Life and Health to me:
Exceedingly thy Word I prize,
The Fund where heav'nly Treasure lies.

Thy Testimonies are my Food,
The saving Oracles of God:
Studious of them on Earth I'll be,
And then fly up to reign with thee.

SALVATION RECOVERED FOR MAN BY JESUS CHRIST

(Isaiah 52:1, 2, 3, 9, 10, 11, 15)

Zion awake, put on thy Strength,
  Resume thy beautiful Array;
The promis'd Saviour comes at length
  To chase thy Guilt and Grief away:
Thee for his Purchase God shall own,
And save thee by his dying Son.

Jerusalem, be holy now,
  Satan no more shall dwell in Thee;
Wash'd from the Sin, and white as Snow,
  Prepare thy God made Man to see;
Prepare Immanuel to behold,
And hear his peaceful Message told.

Shake off the Dust, arise with speed,
  Too long hast thou a Captive been;
Redemption's near, lift up thine Head,
  And cast away the Chains of Sin;
Forth from thy Prison come, and shake
The Yoke of Bondage from thy Neck.

Tho' ye have sold yourselves for nought,
  And forfeited your Claim to Heav'n,
Accept of proffer'd Love unbought;
  Your Treason now is all forgiv'n;
My Blood the fallen Race restores,
And saves without desert of your's.

Ye desert Places, sing for Joy;
  Lost Man, your Hymns of Wonder raise;
Let holy Saints invade the Sky,

And ev'ry Altar flame with Praise:
For I, almighty to redeem,
Have comforted *Jerusalem*.

My Arm's made bare for your Defence,
To save my Church from Satan's Pow'r;
Depart, depart, come out from thence,
Defile yourselves with Sin no more:
Be pure, ye Priests who preach my Word,
And bear the Vessels of the LORD.

Look out and see IMMANUEL come
A World to sprinkle with his Blood;
He many Nations shall bring home,
And save them from the Wrath of GOD:
And Earth's remotest Bounds shall see
The great Salvation wrought by me.

THE 8TH CHAPTER OF HOSEA

Set the loud Trumpet to thy Mouth,
  Let all the final Warning hear;
My everlasting Word of Truth
  To high and low alike declare.

Swift as the rav'nous eagle flies
  And darts, impetuous on her Prey,
Shall their victorious Enemies
  Fill *Israel's* Land with pale Dismay.

Then shall they cry to me in vain;
  Tho' ask'd with Tears, no Aid I'll grant,
Because they did my Words disdain,
  And trample on my Covenant.

Me for their God, they will not have,
  Therefore I give them to the Sword:
Your Foes Commission shall receive
  T' avenge my Quarrel, saith the Lord.

Sin is the God whom they adore,
  And Hell-born Lusts their Rulers are:
Th' apostate Land shall feel my Pow'r,
  The Fury of destructive War.

Go, to your Gods, O Israel, go!
  Samaria, to thy Calf apply!
Thy Idols cannot help thee now,
  Nor save thee when Distress is nigh.

When wilt thou turn to me, thy God?
  When wilt thou seek my injur'd Face?
'Till then my Wrath shall drench in Blood
  The harden'd, unbelieving Race.

Ye Fools and Blind, consider this,
Can they be Gods which Hands have made?
On you and on your Images
I'll hurl the Ruin I have said.

Who sow in Sin shall reap in Pain;
My Word shall surely come to pass:
Unnumber'd Mischiefs yet remain,
Th' Avengers of rejected Grace.

To punish their Apostacy,
The Corn shall perish 'ere it rise;
Or what comes up shall only be
A Portion for their Enemies.

For *Israel* waxes worse and worse,
Nor quakes at my tremendous Frown:
Famine and War unite their Force
To bring a sinful People down.

Before the Heathen *Israel* flies;
His boasted Strength is Weakness found:
As when a broken Vessel lies
Slighted and useless on the Ground.

PART II.

Ephraim is up to *Syria* gone
In all the Confidence of Pride:
Alas, he goes to War alone,
Jehovah is not on his Side.

Ephraim in vain the King of Kings
With condescending Pity woo'd;
The fatal Love of earthly Things
Has drawn him from the Love of God.

The fierce Invaders to repel,
   Tho' they have foreign Aid obtain'd,
Yet shall th' ungrateful Nation feel
   The Weight of my avenging Hand.

Since *Ephraim* hath disguis'd his Sin
   Beneath Religion's specious Form,
His very Prayer shall be unclean,
   And hasten, not avert the Storm.

In vain I gave my gracious Law,
   The Treasure of my written Word;
No Beauty there the Wordlings saw,
   Nor priz'd the Message of the LORD:

Wherefore their Cry I will not hear,
   Nor yet accept their Sacrifice;
Unpardon'd Sin pollutes their Pray'r,
   Nor lets it penetrate the Skies.

In *Egypt* they again shall weep;
   I'll visit their Iniquity:
Their Sins I will in Mem'ry keep,
   Because they have forgotten me.

In vain they fence their Cities round,
   In Forts and Ramparts put their Trust:
Their lofty Spires shall kiss the Ground,
   By Light'ning level'd with the Dust.

THE 125TH PSALM

Who, LORD, confide in Thee,
And in thy Faith endure,
Shall as Mount *Sion* be,
Immoveable and sure:
As CHRIST their Rock, unshook, unmov'd;
Of GOD eternally belov'd.

The rising Mountains stand
Around *Jerusalem;*
So JAH's Almighty Hand
Guards us who trust in Him:
We never will of Safety doubt
While GOD shall compass us about.

Ye Souls who stand in GOD,
Whom JESUS' Blood hath bought,
The guilty Sinner's Rod
Shall never be your Lot;
Ye shall not fall, upheld by Grace,
Nor put your Hands to Wickedness.

The Good and Pure in Heart
Jehovah will defend;
Will not from them depart,
But love them to the End:
He will do well, O Saints, to you,
The LORD will never let you go.

But such as will forsake
The happy Path of Peace,
Deceivers that turn back
To their own Wickedness,

The doubled Wrath of God shall feel,
And sink unpardon'd into Hell.

While they who hear his Call,
 And plead a Saviour's Blood,
Shall reign in Joy with all
 The ransom'd ones of God:
Peace upon *Israel* shall come,
To endless Glory gather'd home.

MATTHEW 6:9–13

Our holy Father, all thy Will
We fain would perfectly fulfil;
But each hast left thy Law undone,
Unworthy to be call'd thy Son.

Who art in Heav'n, enthron'd on high,
Diffusing Glory through the Sky;
Reigning above, on Earth rever'd,
By Saints belov'd, by Sinners fear'd.

For ever hallow'd be thy Name,
The unknown God, the bright I AM;
At which seraphic Choirs, and all
The Hosts of Heaven, prostrate fall.

Thy Kingdom come, ev'n now we wait
Thy Glory to participate:
Rule in our Hearts, unrival'd reign,
Nor e'er withdraw thyself again.

Thy Will, thy Law, thy Precept giv'n,
Be done on earth as 'tis in Heav'n:
Faithful as Angels, fain would we
With cover'd Faces wait on Thee.

Great God, on whom the Ravens cry
For Sustenance, our Wants supply:
Give us this Day, and evermore,
Our daily Bread from Hour to Hour.

Forgive whate'er we do amiss,
Our wilful Sins and Trespasses,
As we forgive (reward us thus)
All them that trespass against us.

And lead us not by Bounty's Tide
Into Temptation, Lust, or Pride:
But what by Mercy we obtain,
Let Pow'r omnipotent restrain.

And O! deliver us, thine own,
From Evil and the Evil one,
Who fain his Darts in us would sheathe,
And bind us with the Chains of Death.

Thou, LORD, canst vanquish his Design,
Thine is the Kingdom, only thine:
The Pow'r, th' eternal Majesty,
And Glory, appertain to thee.

THE 63RD PSALM

O God, my God thou art,
My Father too by Grace:
I dare not from my Hope depart,
Or cease to seek thy Face:

My thirsty Spirit pants
Thy Plenitude to prove,
And comprehend, with all thy Saints,
The Fullness of thy Love.

In this dry, barren Land,
Where Water is not found,
I fain would fly to thy Right Hand,
Where living Streams abound:

Thee, Thee I long to know,
Athirst for God I am,
And come to thee as needy now
As when at first I came.

Thy Glory and thy Pow'r
I long again to see,
To have again, as heretofore,
Sweet Fellowship with thee;

Again to feel thy Peace,
Again thy Name to Praise,
Better than Life thy Favour is,
To all that know thy Grace.

With persevering Hope
Thy Mercy I'll proclaim,
My Hands in steady Faith lift up,
And magnify thy Name:

Thy Praises I'll reveal,
'Till I from Earth remove,
My Mouth with joyful Lips shall tell
The Wonders of thy Love.

PART II.

Surely I Reason have
On thee, my God, to trust;
My Life thou liftest from the Grave,
My Spirit from the Dust:

Thy Grace and boundless Might
My Theme by Day shall be,
My Glory in the silent Night
To meditate on thee.

My Succour thou hast been
When ev'ry Helper fail'd,
Or I, e're now, had fell by Sin,
And Satan had prevail'd;

My Soul, redeem'd from Death,
To thee her Off'ring brings,
And hides her helpless Head beneath
The Covert of thy Wings.

Thou keep'st my steady Feet
In thy appointed Road;
By all the Pow'rs of Hell beset,
I follow after God:

In Jesus I am safe,
My Castle of Resort;
His Hand is both my Shield and Staff,
My Shelter and Support.

The Men who seek to tread
Thy faithful People down,
And persecute, in them, their Head,
And crucify thy Son,

Thou, LORD, will surely foil
In thy avenging Day,
And give their Bodies for a Spoil
To ev'ry Beast of Prey.

But me, and all who love
Thy Worship and thy Ways,
Thou far from Danger wilt remove,
And hide us in thy Place:

Who speak the Words of Truth,
Thou, LORD, on them shalt smile,
But thou wilt stop the Liar's Mouth,
And slay the Sons of Guile.

PSALM 119:41–49

Let thy loving Mercy, LORD,
Come also unto me;
Now, according to thy Word,
My present Saviour be:
Unbelievers then no more
Shall against my Hope blaspheme;
Forc'd to own, "the mighty Pow'r
Of GOD hath rescu'd Him."

In thy Word my Trust I place,
And humbly urge my Claim,
'Till I of thy saving Grace
A living Witness am:
Give, me, LORD, thyself to know,
I shall then thy Law fulfil,
Walk in all Things here below
According to thy Will.

Seeking now in stedfast Faith
I wait a Word from Thee;
Bring my Feet into the Path
Of perfect Liberty;
Then, when I the Path have found,
Unasham'd thy Truth I'll shew:
Kings shall hear the joyful Sound,
And seek Salvation too.

My Delight is in thy Word
Which I have lov'd of old;
Dearer is thy Promise, LORD,
To me than Mines of Gold:
Up to Thee my Hands I lift
'Till I of thy Grace receive;
Give the never-changing Gift,
Thy full Redemption give.

A CONTEMPLATION[1]

(Revelation 7:9–17)

I saw, and lo! a countless throng,
Th' Elect of ev'ry Nation, Name, and Tongue,
Assembled round the everlasting Throne;
With Robes of White endu'd
(The Righteousness of God);
And each a Palm sustain'd
In his victorious Hand;
When thus the bright melodious Choir begun:
"Salvation to thy Name,
Eternal God, and co-eternal Lamb,
In Pow'r, in Glory, and in Essence, One!"

So sung the Saints. Th' angelic Train
Second the Anthem with a loud *Amen*
(These in the outer Circle stood,
The Saints were nearest God);
And prostrate fall, with Glory overpow'r'd,
And hide their Faces with their Wings,
And thus address the King of Kings:
"All hail, by thy triumphant Church ador'd!
Blessing and Thanks and Honour too
Are thy supreme, thy everlasting Due,
Our Triune Sov'reign, our propitious Lord!"

While I beheld th' amazing Sight,
A Seraph pointed to the Saints in White,
And told me who they were, and whence they came;
"These are they, whose Lot below
Was Persecution, Pain, and Woe:
These are the chosen purchas'd Flock,
Who ne'er their Lord forsook:

1 This poem was revised in after years; we give the latter version.

Through his imputed Merit free from Blame;
Redeem'd from ev'ry Sin;
And, as thou seest, whose Garments were made clean,
Wash'd in the Blood of yon exalted Lamb.

Sav'd by his Righteousness alone,
Spotless they stand before the Throne,
And in th' etherial Temple chant his Praise:
Himself among them deigns to dwell,
And Face to Face his Light reveal:
Hunger and Thirst, as heretofore,
And Pain, and Heat, they know no more,
Nor need, as once, the Sun's prolific Rays.
Immanuel, here, his People feeds,
To Streams of Joy perennial leads,
And wipes, for ever wipes, the tears from ev'ry Face."

Happy the Souls releas'd from Fear,
And safely landed there!
Some of the shining Number, once, I knew,
And travell'd with them here:
Nay, some (my elder Brethren now)
Set later out for Heav'n; my junior Saints, below:
Long after me, they heard the Call of Grace
Which wak'd them unto Righteousness.
How have they got beyond!
Converted last, yet first with Glory crown'd!
Little, once, I thought that these
Would first the Summit gain,
And leave me far behind, slow journeying through the Plain.

Lov'd while on Earth; nor less belov'd, tho' gone
Think not I envy you your Crown:
No; if I could, I would not call you down.

Tho' slower is my Pace,
To you I'll follow on,
Leaning on Jesus all the Way,
Who, now and then, lets fall a Ray
Of Comfort from his Throne.
The Shinings of his Grace
Soften my Passage thro' the Wilderness,
And Vines, nectareous, spring where Briers grew:
The sweet Unveilings of his Face
Make me, at times, near half as blest as you.
O, might his Beauty feast my ravish'd Eyes,
His gladd'ning Presence ever stay,
And cheer me all my Journey thro'!
But soon the Clouds return; my Triumph dies;
Damp Vapours from the Valley rise,
And hide the Hill at Sion from my View.

Spirit of Light; thrice holy Dove,
Brighten my Sense of Int'rest in that Love
Which knew no Birth, and never shall expire!
Electing Goodness, firm and free,
My whole Salvation hangs on thee,
Eldest and fairest Daughter of Eternity.
Redemption, Grace, and Glory too,
Our Bliss above, and hopes below,
From her, their Parent-Fountain flow.
Ah, tell me, Lord, that thou hast chosen *me!*
Thou, who hast kindled my intense desire,
Fulfil the Wish thy Influence did inspire,
And let me my Election know!
Then, when thy Summons bids me come up higher,
Well pleas'd I shall from Life retire,
And join the burning Hosts, beheld at distance now.

THE 15TH PSALM

Who, Lord, thy glorious Face shall see,
And reign eternally with Thee?
The Man whose ev'ry Word and Thought
Is modell'd as his Saviour taught:

Whose courteous Lips and guiltless Mouth,
Like His, are full of Grace and Truth;
Whose cautious, inoffensive Tongue
Abhors to do his Neighbour wrong:

Of Saints opprest the Part he'll take,
And love them for their Master's Sake:
Himself impartial to condemn,
And lowly in his own Esteem:

True to his Promise and his Trust,
Strictly and uniformly just:
Whose righteous Hands a Bribe abhor,
Nor take advantage of the Poor.

Whoever thus his Lord obeys,
Holy, like Him, in all his Ways,
Shall never share the Sinner's Doom,
Nor into Condemnation come.

HYMNS OF INVITATION

Again, he limiteth a certain Day, saying in David,—To Day if ye will hear his Voice, harden not your Hearts.—Hebrews 4:7.

SINNER, COME UP WITH ME

Sinner, come up with me,
Here fix thy weeping Eye:
Ascend, in Heart to Calvary,
And see IMMANUEL die.

O bathe with Magdalen
His sacred Feet with Tears:
By Faith embrace thy Master slain
With Sorrow great as Hers.

The Victim bled for thee,
Slight not his dying Cries:
The precious Blood he shed must be
Thy Passport to the Skies.

O tarry not, make Haste,
Ensure thy Claim to Heav'n:
Up! trim thy Lamp! Love much, who hast
So much to be forgiv'n!

LISTEN! THE SAVIOUR CALLS TO THEE

Listen! the Saviour calls to thee,
He bids thee to a Feast:
"Ye weary Sinners, come to Me,
And I will give you Rest."

Thy Maker speaks, incline your Ear,
Thou can'st not hear Enough!
The Joys of Heav'n to Earth prefer,
And turn at his Reproof.

The dying God his Call repeats
To leave the Path of Sin;
And Wisdom, standing at her Gates,
Invites thee to come in.

How long shall Jesus be denied,
And Mercy plead in vain?
His Spirit will not ever chide,
Nor always strive with Man.

Come, and his Glory thou shalt know,
And Live if thou Obey:
Behold th' accepted Time is now,
And this Salvation's Day.

Ev'n now he stands to make thee clean,
His choicest Gifts to give.
He waits to save thee from thy Sin,
And bids thee now Believe.

Believe, and thou shalt surely feel
The Bliss of Sin forgiv'n;
Be rescu'd from the Fear of Hell,
And take thy Seat in Heav'n.

YE SERVANTS OF WOE

Ye Servants of Woe,
  Whom Satan hath bound,
The Father for you
  A Ransom hath found:
Without Variation
  His Word is the Same,
And offers Salvation
  Through Faith in the Lamb.

Redemption from Sin
  This Moment receive;
No longer Unclean,
  In JESUS Believe:
GOD's infinite Anger
  Ye then shall not feel;
He frees you from Danger
  And saves you from Hell.

To JESUS make Haste,
  Accept your Release;
Come, Sinner, and taste
  How gracious he is:
His Blood fully cleanses,
  He shed it for thee,
And bore thy Offences
  When nail'd to the Tree.

That thou mightest claim
  An Heav'nly Crown,
He went as a Lamb
  His Life to lay down:
The Victim was offer'd,
  And pour'd out his Blood!
The Guiltless hath suffer'd,
  To bring us to GOD.

Ev'n now he invites
  Each Sinner to prove,
The endless Delights
  That flow from his Love:
To lift us to Heaven
  Our Advocate stands;
The Nails have engraven
  A World on his Hands.

FOR THE SACRAMENT

Draw near with Faith, ye doubting Souls,
'Tis the Redeemer calls you Home:
His Blood invites all Sinners here,
And cries, incessant, "there is Room."

This, as Himself Commandment left,
In Mem'ry of his Suff'rings do:
Yield up to Him your grateful Hearts,
Who gave his own to bleed for you.

See your inviting Saviour stands,
Able and willing to redeem:
He offers you abundant Life,
And bids you freely come to Him.

Accept at this all-gracious Time,
The Charter of your Sins forgiv'n:
Gird up your Loins, forego the World,
And, leaving Earth, ascend to Heav'n.

Renew your Covenant with God,
Proclaim eternal War with Sin;
See there, your Lord's extended Arms
Are open to receive you in.

This, his last Legacy of Love,
With humble Thankfulness receive:
He came, he died—for us Himself
He gave, and more he could not give.

Dare ev'ry Foe, press through the Crowd;
Your Saviour's Promise call to Mind:
Still keep the Way that leads to God,
Nor dread the Frowns of all Mankind.

Tho' ev'ry Step is pav'd with Snares,
Yet will we to the Skies press on,
And trust each other's Face to see
When gather'd round our Father's Throne.

YOUR LAMPS, YE FOOLISH VIRGINS, TRIM

Your Lamps, ye foolish Virgins, trim,
While it is call'd to-Day;
Arise, the flying Hours redeem,
Sleep not, but Watch and Pray:
Nor proffer'd Mercy thus refuse,
A Moment is too much to lose.

Slack not, but beg to be forgiv'n,
Before your Lot is cast,
Lest, while ye slightly aim at Heav'n,
Ye miss the Mark at last:
Accept, while God the Offer makes,
And climb the Rock that never shakes.

Why should terrestrial Things engross
Th' affections due to God?
Break off your Sins, the deadly Foes
That shed Jehovah's Blood:
From Sodom flee, escape its Pains,
While yet your Day of Grace remains.

Fall at his Feet with humble Fear,
And he shall bid you rise,
Shall change your guilty Nature here,
And fit you for the Skies:
This is his Will concerning you,
That where he is ye may be too.

Hath Satan giv'n a sleeping Draught,
And so become your Lord?
Or has he shot a poison'd Shaft,
And are your Wounds uncur'd?

To JESUS fly, the living Stream,
And find your Antidote in Him.

Still, should he seem to hide his Face,
The Pray'r of Faith repeat;
He surely will display his Grace,
And make the Cure complete:
Shall cause you in his Ways to stand,
Then seat you at his own right Hand.

TO MR. S.M.

With eager Haste let others strive
To keep the Joys of Sense alive,
 Neglecting those of Heav'n:
But let my Friend, with Views sublime,
Know that his Talents and his Time
 For nobler Ends were giv'n.

Superior to *their* Pleasures live;
To JESUS look and wisely give
 Your blooming Hours to *Him:*
Thy Care to shun his dread Reproof,
While others deem it *Wit* to scoff,
 Politeness to Blaspheme.

Defy their Frown, their Smile despise,
Look upwards to the radiant Prize
 That waits the Saints above:
With zealous Faith pursue the Lamb;
An Int'rest in his Merit claim,
 An Int'rest in his Love.

High on a Precipice we go,
And ev'ry Breath we draw below
 With Danger pregnant is:
Yet, trifling as our Moments seem,
Our endless State depends on Them,
 Eternal Woe or Bliss.

Up, then, my Friend, pursue thy Way;
Short is Life's momentary Day,
 And Night is coming on:
We shall not, in our final Hour,

Complain we made our Pardon sure
  Or knew our God too soon.

Did Monck repeat his happy Choice,
When Death, with unexpected Voice,
  Pronounc'd his Call to Heav'n?
How dreadful had the Summons been
If it had found him still in Sin,
  Unholy, uuforgiv'n?

Young as thou art, thou too *may'st* fall
His early Prey who conquers all,
  Arrested in thy Bloom:
Say, could'st thou run thy Lord to meet,
With Joy thy Soul to him commit,
  The Body to the Tomb?

While Jesus here thy Virtue tries,
May Sin, with its delusive Joys,
  Far from thy Breast be driv'n:
Untasted pass Earth's Follies by,
And, fill'd with God, may'st thou and I
  Walk Hand in Hand to Heav'n!

LIFE AND IMMORTALITY BROUGHT TO LIGHT BY THE GOSPEL

How blest am I! no Snare I fear
While Jesus keeps his Dwelling here:
His Presence chases Death away,
Enliv'ning with continual Day.

By Satan's Rage I stand unshook,
My Hopes are founded on a Rock:
Christ is the Stone on which I build,
My Castle, Guardian, Helmet, Shield!

O ye, who ransack Vice for Bliss,
Draw near and taste how good he is:
Your Pardon thankfully receive,
Eat of the Tree of Life and live.

No longer naming Seraphs ward,
Or stand the hallow'd Fruit to guard;
Your Saviour's Death broke down the Wall;
Then hear Him, and obey his Call.

Returning Sinner, why afraid?
Dry up thy Tears, thy Ransom's paid:
Jesus proclaims thy Liberty,
Who died to purchase Life for Thee.

Empty'd of all *Self*-Righteousness,
By Faith assume and put on His:
The Crown by Him so dearly bought,
Costs the believing Sinner nought.

TO MR. E. W.

(March, 1757)

Soldier of the Living God,
  Steward of the mystic Word,
Use the Gifts by Him bestow'd
  To the Honour of thy Lord:
Free thou did'st from Him receive,
Man of God as freely give.

Clad with Zeal as with a Cloak,
  Boldly urge thy rapid Way;
Rooted, grounded in the Rock,
  Faithful in the trying Day:
Stand in Jesus thine Abode,
Safely hid with Him in God.

In Immanuel's Strength go forth,
  Wrestle with Contempt and Shame;
Dare the feeble Sons of Earth,
  Conquer in his saving Name:
March with Jesus for thy Guide,
Go, for God is on thy Side!

Bear the Standard of the Lord,
  Fight thy Captain's Battles well;
By the Spirit's two-edged Sword
  Put to flight the Hosts of Hell:
Single thou thy Foes shalt chase,
Arm'd with all the Strength of Grace.

Satan and the World may join,
  Hell and Death with thee engage,
Thou art strong in Strength Divine,
  Safe amidst their blackest Frown.

Jesus shall thy Soul confirm,
Lift thee up above the Storm.

Vainly shall the blinded Crew
  Strive thy Progress to withstand;
Thee they never shall subdue,
  Guarded by the Saviour's Hand:
God hath said concerning Thee,
"As thy Day thy Strength shall be."

But if Jesus should depart,
  For a Season cease to smile,
Proving what is in thine Heart,
  Leave thee to thyself a while,
He again thy Stay will prove,
Bear thee in his Arms of Love.

When thou dost in secret Pray'r
  Find a ready, free Access,
When thou tellest all thy Care
  Sweetly at the Throne of Grace,
Me to Jesus then commend,
Think upon thy distant Friend!

Fix on Christ thy single Eye,
  His be thine, and all thou art;
Ev'ry Moment keep Him nigh,
  Never from his Side depart:
This thy sure and constant Aim,
Enoch-like, to walk with Him.

Dauntless thou his Word proclaim,
  Tell his Message to Mankind;
Bid them, in thy Master's Name,
  Take the Pearl for them design'd;

Tell them JESUS will redeem
All that come to GOD by Him.

Faithful to thy sacred Trust,
  Thus from Strength to Strength go on:
Stay the Weak, bring back the Lost,
  Labour till thy Work is done:
Fight and Conquer, end the Strife,
Then assume Eternal Life.

OCCASIONAL PIECES ON THE DEATH OF FRIENDS

Whosoever liveth and believeth in me shall never die.
—John 11:26.

——*Quid sibi Saxa cavata,*
Quid pulchra volunt Monumenta,
Nisi quòd Res creditur illis
Non mortua, sed data Somno?
—Prudentius

EPITAPH ON MRS. E. B.

If Candour, Merit, Sense, or Virtue dies,
Reader, beneath thy Feet dead Virtue lies,
Yet still she lives, if Worth can eternize:
Lives, far above the Reach of Death: But where?
In Heav'n, and ev'ry Heart that knew her here.
Vain are Encomiums; Praise is idly spent
On them whose Actions are their Monument.
    Thrice sacred Tomb, be loyal to thy Trust,
And guard, 'till CHRIST revives her hallow'd Dust:
Then, as a faithful Steward, safe restore
The precious Treasure thou must keep no more.

EPITAPH ON MR. G. WALTON

The Debt of Nature I have paid,
  Which thou must shortly pay:
To learn Instruction from the Dead,
  Thou breathing Taper, stay.

Swifter than Thought thy Years depart,
  My Verse proclaims their Haste:
A Moment nearer Death thou art
  Than when you read the last.

Soon must thy Earth to Earth be giv'n,
  Soon must thou disappear:
Say, Reader, is thy Heart in Heav'n,
  And is thy Treasure there?

Like Thee the prostrate Dead I view'd,
  While in the Flesh detain'd:
How differ we? Thou'rt on the Road,
  I've reach'd my Journey's End.

ON THE DEATH OF MR. T. M.

Sweet Youth, sleep calmly on,
For, lo! thy Work is done;
Sleep, while Flow'rs thy Grave surround,
Screen it with their verdant shade,
Carpet the enamel'd Ground,
Mark the Place where thou art laid.

Let Nature, Day by Day,
Her Flow'ry Tribute pay:
Clad with unaccustom'd Bloom
Let the sacred Earth appear;
By the Verdure of thy Tomb,
Shew that thou art slumb'ring there.

The Grave does but secure
And make thy Glory sure:
Find in this thy safe Retreat
From the Rage of Fiends and Men,
Call'd to take thine early Seat
With the Saviour at Eighteen!

Learned, yet sweetly mild,
Meek as a little Child;
To thy Maker's Will resign'd,
Blest with plain Simplicity:
All the Saviour's humble Mind,
Gentlest Wisdom shone in Thee.

Arm'd with IMMANUEL'S Name,
He more than overcame:
Strengthen'd in the inner Man,
Fill'd with all the Spirit's Might;

Borne on Wings of outward Pain
 To the peaceful Realms of Light,

 Try'd to the utmost here,
 We hail Him enter'd there:
He with Foes unnumber'd strove,
 Forc'd his glorious Passage through
Finish'd all the Work of Love,
 Giv'n Him by God to do.

 And shall thy Friends lament,
 Or mourn thy blest Ascent?
Grieve that thou hast conquer'd Death,
 Took Possession of thy Throne?
Nay! but let them wear thy Wreath,
 Make thy Heav'nly Joys their own!

 Forbid your tears to flow,
 Grief were *unfriendly* now:
Weeping Throng, remain assur'd
 Righteous is the Will of God;
Say, with *Eli*, "'Tis the Lord,
 Let him do as seems him good!"

 He is not *Dead*, but *Sleeps*,
 Th' eternal Sabbath keeps;
Elevate above the Sky,
 Waits on his etherial King:
Heav'nly Hymns his Voice employ,
 Such as brightest Angels sing.

 Would ye his Bliss attain,
 And see your Friend again?
At his high Perfection aim,
 Manfully your Foes resist:

Be ye Followers of Him,
    Even as he follow'd CHRIST.

His Footsteps meekly trace,
    And run a faithful Race:
Imitate the Saint ye mourn,
    Then, like Him, from Earth retire;
From the World by Seraphs borne,
    Meet Him in the upper Choir.

    Shall I with Him appear
    In heav'nly Mansions there?
JESUS, bear me safe beneath
    Through a World of Sin and Strife:
Make me faithful unto Death,
    Then bestow the Crown of Life!

ON THE DEATH OF MRS. F. T.

(June 3, 1754)

There remaineth therefore a Rest to the People of God.—HEBREWS 4:9.

The Robes of Light our Sister wears,
 Which emulate the Sun,
Should cause us to suspend our Tears,
And make our Anthems rival theirs
 Who stand before the Throne.

Glory to Him whose Love constrains,
 And saves us by his Blood:
By Virtue of his dying Pains
She finds the Rest that still remains
 For ev'ry Child of GOD.

In fiery Trials Day by Day
 Unshaken did she stand:
To Glory sweetly made her Way,
Meek and resign'd, as passive Clay
 In her great Potter's Hand.

Her Woes their Period have found,
 They cannot now enslave,
Nor come where endless Joys abound,
Nor haunt her peaceful Soul beyond
 The Limit of the Grave.

Victorious she assumes the Wreath
 For Conquerors design'd,
The End of persevering Faith;
And leaves her Cares, releas'd by Death,
 Eternally behind.

No more, by Satan's Rage pursued,
 Affliction shalt thou see;

Secure of Heav'n for thine Abode,
Blest with the Presence of thy God
    To all Eternity.

The Happy Change that Life deny'd,
    Assisting Death affords;
Behold her at Immanuel's Side,
Unutterably glorify'd,
    Immutably the Lord's!

O may we too maintain our Ground,
    From Faith to Faith go on!
At the last Day in Christ be found,
And form the Circles that surround
    His everlasting Throne!

ON THE DEATH OF THE RIGHT HONOURABLE WILLIAM, EARL OF HARRINGTON

(Dec. 9, 1756)

How shall my Pen, with proper Force, reveal
The Grief in vain I labour to conceal?
Where shall my Muse at STANHOPE's Praise begin,
Too great for Speech, too vast to keep within?
Assist, dread *Melpomene*, my Design,
That solemn Energy may fill each Line:
Aid me to sing the Honours of his Name
In Terms proportion'd to so great a Theme!

Britain, weep on; let Floods with Floods combine,
While fair *Hibernia* adds her Tears to thine:
That faithful Partner renders Groan for Groan,
Partakes thy Pangs, nor lets thee weep alone.

Tho' *France* no more shall suffer by his Steel,
The Blows receiv'd she will for ever feel;
Her Envy and her Terror once who stood,
No more shall dye his Sword in *Gallic* Blood:
Yet ev'n in Death a Conqu'ror he appears,
Exchanging Laurels for a Diadem of Stars.

Yes, HARRINGTON: Methinks I see thee rise,
Upborne, to Glory on the People's Sighs:
As widow'd Sisters, lo! in awful State
Three sympathizing Kingdoms wail thy Fate,
With martial Heat who formerly wert fir'd,
Abroad tremendous, and at Home admir'd;
Astonish'd Thee, *Britannia's* Foes beheld,
Wise in the Senate, dreadful in the Field,
True to thy Monarch, prudent, cautious, just,
And faithful to thy each important Trust.

When *England's* great Affairs on thee were laid,
Thy Wisdom shone, thy Conduct was display'd:
So Palms, the more weigh'd down, the higher rise,
And shoot their loaded Branches to the Skies.
Live then for ever, take th' unfading Wreath,
And look with Scorn on Courts and Things beneath;
While *British* Chronicles and high Renown
Embalm the Name of deathless HARRINGTON.

ON THE DEATH OF MR. ENOCH WILLIAMS

(August, 1757)

And ENOCH walked with GOD. He was not, for GOD took Him.

—GENESIS 5:24.

Hearken! the Saviour's Voice at last
Invites his Suff'rer home,
And tells thee all thy Toil is past,
But thy Reward is come.

'Till meet for Bliss on Earth detain'd,
The Conquest thou hast won;
Through much Temptation, thou hast gain'd
The Prize, and reach'd the Crown.

While shouting Angels chaunt their Joys,
And tune their Notes the higher,
And clap their Wings, for O! thy Voice
Is added to their Choir.

Of his Inheritance above
They hail a Saint possest:
Made meet, by his Redeemer's Love,
To be Jehovah's Guest.

Swift as an Arrow through the Air
The tow'ring Spirit flies,
Intrusted to a Seraph's Care,
And convoy'd to the Skies:

On the expanded Wings of Love
He seeks his high Abode,
To meet the happy Souls above,
His Zeal brought home to GOD.

Him they salute with lifted Cry
As soon as entered there,

"But for thy favour'd Ministry,
Or we had not been here:

From Pain to Glory summon'd forth,
Thrice welcome from below,
Our Fellow-sufferer on Earth,
Our Fellow-angel now!"

While humbly he draws near the Throne,
The Saviour's crystal Seat;
Gives him the Praise, and casts his Crown
At His redeeming Feet.

Lifted above the Reach of Pain,
We soon shall change our Place;
And join IMMANUEL's shining Train,
And see his blissful Face.

Rejoicing in that glorious Hope,
We bear his Cross below;
We quickly shall be taken up,
Sublimer Joys to know.

For *our* Arrival into Bliss
Our Friends in Glory wait:
Cut short thy Work in Righteousness,
And make their Joys complete!

The happy Soul whom JESUS gives
In Him to Live and Die,
It's blest Transition scarce perceives
Into Eternity.

A Sight of Him that conquer'd Death
In our last Moments giv'n,

Shall elevate our languid Faith,
And charm us into Heav'n.

CHRIST when expiring *Stephen* view'd,
He scorn'd Death's utmost Pow'r,
And calmly fell asleep in GOD
Amidst the stony Show'r.

Assist us, LORD, to walk and live
In *Sion's* balmy Road,
And then our Souls to Thee receive
When call'd to meet our GOD.

A little while and we shall soar
To yonder promis'd Land,
And meet our Breth'ren gone before
Enthron'd at thy Right Hand:

Thy Praise shall actuate each Tongue,
Thy Love our Hearts enflame;
And we with them shall sing the Song
Of *Moses* and the Lamb.

EPITAPH ON MASTER EUSTACE BATEMAN

Hail, happy Youth, so early taken home,
Caught up by JESUS from the Ill to come:
By thy Redeemer sweetly order'd hence,
E're Vice had marr'd thy spotless Innocence.

When twice six Winters he had scarcely seen,
His Heav'n-born Soul disdain'd to dwell with Men:
Ardent the Crown eternal to receive,
And ripe for Heav'n, he only Died to Live.

ON THE DEATH OF THE REVD. MR. R. B.

Let me die the Death of the Righteous, and let my last End be like His.—Numbers 23:10.

Thrice happy they who sleep in God,
Securely wafted o'er the Flood
  To *Canaan's* peaceful Shore!
Whose Lives were as a daily Death,
Who walk'd with God, and liv'd by Faith,
  And now shall die no more!

Such, gracious Lord, we wish to be;
Such was our Pastor, now with thee,
  Our Candlestick below:
A burning and a shining Light
He liv'd a while to bless our Sight,
  But shines in Glory now.

A Prophet hallow'd from the Womb,
To seek and bring the Wand'rers home
  Anointed, set apart:
Enabled by the searching Word
To set the Message of the Lord
  Home to the Sinner's Heart.

His ev'ry Pow'r devoted was
To further his Redeemer's Cause;
  Nor did his Talents hide:
A Beacon set upon a Hill,
He liv'd to do his Master's Will,
  He did his Will, and died.

A faithful Messenger he stood,
The Trumpet and the Mouth of God
  To make his Counsel known:
His Life one constant Voice hath been,

Inviting Sinners to come in,
And claim th' eternal Crown.

May I like Him my Hours employ,
Finish, like Him, my Course with Joy,
And sleep to wake in Bliss!
Like Him be number'd with the blest!
JESUS, regard my one Request,
Make my last End like His.

ON THE DEATH OF MR. R. V.

Be not slothful, but Followers of them who, through Faith and Patience, inherit the Promises.—HEBREWS 6:12.

The Crown of Righteousness is giv'n,
Our friend is landed safe in Heav'n:
His Warfare now accomplish'd is,
And Face to Face his LORD he sees.

For ever now redeem'd from Pain,
He did not run nor strive in vain:
With Triumph from his Clay releas'd,
Translated to his Place of Rest.

Ear hath not heard, nor Eye beheld
What to the Saints is there reveal'd:
Blissful Experience only knows
The Glories of the upper House.

Far, far from all Distress remov'd,
They *know* the GOD whom here they lov'd:
Temptation, Sickness, Grief, and Care,
Shall never gain Admission there.

Then let us seek, in steadfast Faith,
A City that Foundations hath:
Our bright, immoveable Abode,
Whose glorious Architect is GOD.

There we shall all our Pain forget,
And only Songs of Praise repeat;
In Knowledge, Happiness, and Love,
To all Eternity improve.

There we shall as the Angels shine,
The Martyr's noble Army join;

And see the Lamb (thrice blissful sight!)
Encompass'd with his Saints in Light.

When shall we to our Joy be giv'n?
O, when exchange this Earth for Heav'n,
And cast our Crowns before the Throne,
And worship Him that sits thereon?

When shall we hear th' inviting Word,
And be for ever with the LORD?
A Day with CHRIST in Glory there
Is better than a Thousand here.

Holy and True call in thine own;
Accomplish, LORD, their Number soon:
Us to thy second Coming seal,
And with thyself for ever fill!

AN APPENDIX

Consisting of several PIECES not properly reducible to any of the preceding HEADS.

LOOK BACK, MY SOUL, AND TAKE A VIEW

Look back, my Soul, and take a View
  Of God expiring on the Tree:
Behold Jehovah breathe his Last,
  To buy eternal Life for thee!
Thy Maker faints—"'Tis finish'd," cries,
Reclines his sacred Head, and dies.

Shadows and Types are done away,
  The Temple's Veil is rent in twain:
Vanish, ye emblematic Rites,
  The *real* Victim now is slain;
Is slain for Sinners to atone,
The Priest and Sacrifice in one.

Methinks I see the purpled Earth
  Startle to feel its Maker's Blood;
The Sun retires, and from their Graves
  Saints rise to hail their dying God:
Each sympathizing Rock appears
More tender than His Murderers.

And did the Saviour thus exchange
  His Throne of Glory for a Cross?
Left he for this th' etherial Court,
  To die a painful Death for us?
For us he bled at ev'ry Vein,
And, slain *by* Man, *for* Man was slain!

Obdurate Heart, shall Mountains heave,
  And Nature mourn her best-belov'd?
Shall e'en Rocks shudder at the Sight,
  And I alone abide unmov'd?

Shall I not weep his Death to see
Who wept in Tears of Blood for me?

O, Prince of Martyrs, touch my Heart!
  There let thy mighty Standard rest;
Burn purifying Incense there,
  Fit it for so divine a Guest:
There let thy pow'rful Cross reside
'Till ev'ry Lust is crucify'd.

TO A FRIEND WHO ASK'D WHAT GOD IS

Is there a Man whose daring Hand
Can number ev'ry Grain of Sand?
Can count the Drops that fill the Sea,
Or tell how many Stars there be?

Who, then, shall strive to comprehend
Infinity that knows no End?
Who shall set Bounds to boundless Pow'r,
Restrain Omnipotence, or lower
Eternity to one poor Hour?

Believe me, Friend, thou can'st no more
The vast Designs of God explore,
Than thy short Arm can touch the Skies,
Or fathom Ocean's deep Abyss.

Who shall disclose his Maker's Plan,
Or dare his secret Will to scan?
Shall feeble, guilty, finite Man?

None but Perfection such as His,
Can know th' Almighty as he is,
His Glory never can be brought
Adapted to a Mortal's Thoughts.

His Majesty we can't discern,
His Attributes we cannot learn,
'Till Death removes our fleshly Glass,
And shows his Glory Face to Face.

God is a Theme too great for Thought;
An awful Something, who knows what?
Be silent, and submit to show
Respect to what thou must not know.

Consider what thou art, and fear
This unseen Witness always near;
Dive not into his deep Decree:
The Objects too elate for thee,
Thou must not ask, nor wish to see.

Cast each presumptuous Doubt away;
Remember thou'rt, at best, but Clay,
Whose only Province is t' obey.

REDEEMED OFFENDER, HAIL THE DAY

Behold, I have graven Thee on the Palms of my Hands.
—Isaiah 49:16.

Redeemed Offender, hail the Day
That sees thy Sin forgiv'n:
Jesus hath borne thy Guilt away,
And pleads for thee in Heav'n.

Imprinted on His Hands thou art
In Characters of Blood;
The Stream that issu'd from his Heart
Shall waft thee safe to God.

For me vouchsaf'd th' unspotted Lamb
His Father's Wrath to bear:
I see his Feet, and read my Name
Engraven deeply there.

Forth from the Lord his gushing Blood
In purple Currents ran:
And ev'ry Wound proclaim'd aloud
His wond'rous Love to Man.

My Faith looks back and sees Him bleed;
A Thorny Crown he wears,
To set upon the Sinner's Head
A shining Crown of Stars.

Saviour, I fain wou'd take the Wreath,
To thee, my Centre, move,
In all the Lowliness of Faith,
In all the Heights of Love.

Thy Righteousness my Robe shalt be,
Thy bitter Death my Hope:

For my Offence upon the Tree
My LORD was lifted up.

For me the Saviour's Blood avails,
Almighty to atone:
The Hands he gave to piercing Nails
Shall lead me to his Throne.

CAN MY HEAVEN-BORN SOUL SUBMIT

Be careful for nothing.—PHILIPPIANS 4:6.

Can my Heav'n-born Soul submit
To care for Things below?
Nay, but never from the Feet
Of JESUS may I go:
Anxious, LORD, for nothing Here,
In ev'ry Straight I look to thee;
Humbly cast my ev'ry Care
On Him that cares for me.

Godliness is greatest Gain,
For that alone I pray;
LORD, I never will complain,
Give thou or take away:
Never will I grieve for ought,
So CHRIST is mine and I am His
I will ne'er, by taking Thought,
Obstruct my inward Peace.

He shall dwell in perfect Rest
Whose Mind is stay'd on Thee,
Whom to keep within my Breast
My only Care shall be:
View the Lilies of the Field,
They grow, but neither toil nor spin,
By their Maker's Arm upheld
Who clothes the Earth with Green.

See the Ravens, Day by Day,
Their Maker gives them Food;
Lions, roaring for their Prey,
Do seek their Meat from GOD,
Lean thou on his faithful Word,

Nor, by Distrust, provoke his Wrath:
Cast thy Burden on the LORD,
O Thou of little Faith!

Will the Saviour (who thy Peace
At such a Price hath bought)
From his Work of Mercy cease,
And sell thy Life for nought?
Doubting Soul, to Him look up,
His Ears are open to thy Cry:
GOD can recompense thy Hope,
And all thy Need supply.

Thou hast promis'd Help to Thine.
And I believe the Word;
I will never ask a Sign,
Nor dare to tempt the LORD:
'Tis enough for GOD to say,
I'll feed my People with my Hand;
Heav'n and Earth shall pass away,
But his Decree shall stand.

JUDGMENT

Behold, the awful Day comes on,
When Jesus on his righteous Throne
  Shall in the Clouds appear:
With solemn Pomp shall bow the Sky,
And, in the Twinkling of an Eye,
  Arraign us at his Bar.

But first th' Archangel's Trump shall blow,
Our scatter'd Dust its Voice shall know,
  And quicken at the Sound:
The Sea shall then give up her Dead:
And Nations, starting from their Bed,
  Shall cleave the op'ning Ground.

Who shall sustain his righteous Ire,
When Jesus sets the Clouds on Fire,
  And makes the Earth retreat?
In vain shall Sinners *then* repent,
When each expiring Element,
  Shall melt with fervent Heat.

The Dead in Christ shall first awake,
The faithful few, who, for *his* Sake,
  On Earth were justify'd:
Guarded by a seraphic Band,
Aloft they mount to his Right Hand,
  In whom they liv'd and died.

See next the guilty Crowd arise,
Beholding, with reluctant Eyes,
  The Glories of the Lamb;
While taunting Fiends impatient wait

To hurl them from the Judgment Seat,
  To Hell's eternal Flame.

Hark, as they mount, by Devils borne,
To meet their Judge, (on Earth their Scorn)
  Despairingly they cry,
"Fall on us, Rocks, with all your Load,
And screen us from the Wrath of GOD,
  And hide us from his Eye."

In vain on Rocks and Hills ye call,
The Rocks shall from their Basis fall
  And know their Place no more:
The Hills shall melt when GOD comes down,
And Mountains crumble at his Frown,
  And groan beneath his Pow'r.

What Thought can paint their black Despair,
Who this tremendous Sentence hear,
  Irrevocably giv'n,
"Depart, ye cursed, into Hell,
With everlasting Burnings dwell,
  Remote from me and Heav'n?"

But, O thou Saviour of Mankind,
Display thy Pow'r, and to the Blind
  Effectual Light afford:
Snatch them from Unbelief and Sin,
And *now* compel Them to come in,
  And tremble at thy Word.

Methinks I hear thy Mercy plead,
The Voice of Him that wakes the Dead
  Doth over Sinners mourn:
"Why do ye still your GOD forget,

And madly hasten to the Pit
From whence is no Return"?

"Ye *Reasoners*, make a rational Choice;
Listen, in Time, to Reason's Voice,
Nor dare Almighty Ire:
Turn, lest the hottest Wrath ye feel,
And find, too late, the Flames of Hell
No Metaphoric Fire."

CONTEMPT OF THE WORLD

Can ought below engross my Thoughts?
Or am I to the World confin'd?
Nay, let my pure Affections soar
To Objects of a nobler Kind!

I know I'm but a Pilgrim here
That seeks a better, promis'd Land:
Then may I run and never tire,
'Till that celestial Home's obtain'd.

Resolv'd to tread the sacred Way
That Jesus water'd with his Blood,
I bend my fix'd and cheerful Course
Through that rough Path my Master trod.

Contemptuous of the World I live,
A daily Death rejoice to die:
And, while I move and walk below,
My absent Heart mounts up on High.

O Light of Life, still guide my Steps,
Without thy friendly Aid I stray;
Lead me, my God, for I am blind,
Direct me and point out my Way.

Let the vain World applaud or frown,
Still may I Heaven's Path pursue:
Still may I stand unshook, and keep
The Centre of my Hopes in View!

What is the World's good Word to me,
If by my God from Glory driv'n?
Can that redeem my Soul from Hell,
Or recompence my Loss of Heav'n?

Tho' Satan, Earth, and self oppose,
Yet, through thy Help, I'll persevere;
To *Canaan's* Hills my Eyes lift up,
And choose my Lot and Portion there.

The Way that leads to Glory lies
Through Ill-report, Contempt and Loss:
Assist me to deny myself,
To follow Thee and bear thy Cross.

Let Satan never come between,
Nor separate my God and me;
But may my Soul, in ev'ry Storm,
Find a sure resting Place in Thee.

DYING CREATOR, SLAUGHTERED LAMB

Dying Creator, slaughter'd Lamb,
  Thou poured'st out thy Blood for me;
O may I, kindled by thy Flame,
  As freely give myself to Thee!
My Heart to thee I now resign,
For, LORD, it cost the Blood of thine!

To save my falling Soul from Death
  Th' immaculate Redeemer died;
LORD, my Offences drove the Nails,
  The Soldier, I, that pierc'd thy Side:
For this my restless Eye runs o'er
Because I can lament no more.

How gladly should my Head have worn,
  The Crown of Thorns to hinder Thine!
Have suffer'd in my Master's stead,
  And made thy dying Sorrows mine!
Have stretch'd my Arms upon the Tree,
And died myself to rescue Thee!

But O! no other Sacrifice
  The Father's Justice could appease;
Ten thousand Worlds had died in vain,
  Thy Blood alone could buy our Peace:
The GOD offended must be slain
To expiate the Offence of Man!

And shall I not his Cross take up
  Who died upon a Cross for me?
JESUS, through good and ill-Report,
  I, in thy Strength, will follow thee:

My Master liv'd despis'd, abhorr'd,
And I am not above my Lord.

The World combin'd, with one Consent,
To trample on the Great Supreme;
The very God of very God,
A Man of Sorrows here became,
And all who seek in Heav'n to reign,
Must enter through the Gate of Pain.

FICKLE AND CHANGEABLE IS MAN

Faithful is he that calleth you, who also will do it.—1 THES. 5:24.

Fickle and changeable is Man,
Terrestrial Joys are just as vain,
  And perish in the Tasting;
But JESUS' Truth I cannot fear,
His Gifts without Repentance are,
  His Love is everlasting.

Mercy unchangeable is His,
Eternal as Himself it is,
  Nor will his Promise fail me:
I own the Token he has giv'n,
And steadily press on to Heav'n,
  Tho' Fiends and Men assail me.

He never will from me remove;
For me the Saviour pleads above,
  Still making Intercession:
I hear his Pray'r, I feel his Blood,
Kept by the mighty Pow'r of GOD
  Through Faith unto Salvation.

His Spirit for that End is giv'n,
To bear unhurt, unstain'd to Heav'n
  The Soul of each Believer:
Deputed by the Lamb he is
To comfort, guard, and strengthen His,
  And stay with Them for ever.

Through Him united to the Son,
Unalienably seal'd his own,
  Nor Earth nor Hell shall move me:
From Conqu'ring I to Conquer go:

JESUS hath lov'd me hitherto,
And to the End will love me.

Bent to devour the Serpent stands,
But CHRIST from his own mighty Hands,
Will never let Him force me:
My Maker is my Husband now,
Nor Heights above nor Depths below
Shall from my LORD divorce me.

If, for a Season, Satan's Chain
Be lengthen'd, JESUS will sustain
Me in the sore Temptation;
Will frustrate the Accuser's Hope,
And bear my ransom'd Spirit up
Above the inundation.

His Name assuredly I prove
Essential Faithfulness and Love;
Shall I, by Doubting, grieve Him?
My Soul He with a Price hath bought,
His Law within my Heart is wrote,
And I shall never leave Him.

OCCASIONAL
HYMNS AND POEMS

Composed Between The Years 1760–1778

Collected And Printed,

Without Alteration or Abridgment, from

THE ORIGINALS.

Being the Whole of the Remaining

POETICAL PIECES

OF THE

REV. AUGUSTUS M. TOPLADY, B.A.

I will Praise the name of God with a Song, and will magnify Him with Thanksgiving.—PSALM 69:30.

A MORNING HYMN TO CHRIST

(Imitated from the Latin of Buchanan.)

Offspring of God, whose Birth Divine
  Not Angels can relate;
Co-equal, co-eternal Beam,
  Of Glory uncreate!

Thee, very God of very God,
  And Light of Light we own:
Of God, thy Everlasting Sire,
  The Everlasting Son.

The purple Dawn, with gradual Hand,
  Unveils the Face of Things:
Fast as the Shades of Night retire,
  All Nature smiles and sings.

But deeper Gloom than Midnight wears,
  Involves our sinful Race:
'Till thy bright Beams, ETERNAL SUN,
  The moral Darkness chase.

Error and Sin, to blind our Sight,
  Their ten-fold Curtain spread:
O rise on thy benighted World,
  And give the Day we need!

Icy and dull our Passions are,
  When they to Thee should move;
Diffuse thy Heat, and make us feel
  Th' Attraction of thy Love!

Sin's noxious Damps, and Error's Mist,
  Absorb, and sweep aside:
And bid thy soft, refreshing Dew,
  Into our Bosoms glide.

Then, quicken'd with thy genial Ray,
And water'd with thy Blood,
Our new-born Souls shall flourish fair,
And bring forth Fruit to God.

FAITH TRIUMPHANT

How happy are we
Our Election who see,
And can venture our Souls on thy gracious Decree.
In Jesus approv'd,
From Eternity lov'd,
And lodg'd in his Hand, whence we cannot be mov'd!

'Tis sweet to recline
On the Bosom divine;
And experience the Comforts peculiar to Thine:
While, born from above,
And upheld by thy Love,
We, with Singing and Triumph, to Zion remove.

As Doves, we have prest
To the Ark of thy Breast;
That Harbour of Safety, that Centre of Rest:
Thou hast taken us in;
Thou hast cancell'd our Sin;
And sown the sure Seed of Salvation within.

Our seeking thy Face
Was the Fruit of thy Grace;
Thy Goodness deserves, and shall have all the Praise:
No Sinner can be
Before hand with Thee:
Thy Grace is almighty, preventing, and free.

Effectually drawn,
We came to thy Son;
And thou'lt perfect the Work, for the Work was thy own:
Thy Breath from above

The Spark shall improve;
No Floods can extinguish our Dawning of Love.

Our Saviour and Friend
His Love shall extend;
It knew no Beginning, and never shall End:
Whom once He receives
His Spirit ne'er leaves;
Nor revokes, nor repents of, the Grace that he gives.

Thro' Mercy we taste
The invisible Feast;
The Bread of the Kingdom, the Wine of the Blest:
Who grants us to know
The Foretaste below,
Will endless Salvation and Glory bestow.

This proof we can give,
That Thee we receive,
Thou art precious alone to the Souls that believe:
Thou art precious to Us;
All beside is as Dross,
When compar'd with thy Love and the Blood of thy Cross.

Yet one thing we want;
More HOLINESS grant!
For more of thy Mind and thy Likeness we pant:
Thy Image impress
On thy Favourite Race;
O fashion and polish thy Vessels of Grace!

Thy Workmanship we
More plainly would be;
Lord, take us in hand, and conform us to Thee!

Thy Impression to bear,
Thy Likeness to wear,
Be this our Ambition, our Hope, and our Pray'r!

Thou hast made it our Will
To resemble Thee still:
Turn our Hearts to thy Spirit, as Clay to the Seal!
As nearer we move
To the Canaan above
Make us holy and blameless before Thee in Love.

All this shall be done;
'Tis already begun:
Thou, from conqu'ring to conquer, in us wilt go on.
In us, when we die,
Thy Grace from on high
Will the finishing Hand to thy Image apply.

We shall still be renew'd,
'Till thy Spirit and Blood
Have ripen'd us quite for the Vision of God:
When that Moment is come:
Thou wilt send for us home;
And thy perfected Saints to thy Glory assume.

On IMMANUEL's Land
We shortly shall stand,
With Crowns on our Heads, and with Harps in our Hand:
His Harp, lo, each tunes!
Lo, we cast down our crowns!
And with Songs of Salvation, Heav'n's Concave resounds!

PRAISE FOR CONVERSION

King of Glory, sov'reign God,
Gracious Source of all that's good!
Thou hast made my Soul anew;
Wrought in me to will and do:
On thy Head the Crown I set;
Cast my Honours at thy Feet.

Boasting, Lord, is not for me;
What I am, I am thro' Thee;
Let not me usurp the Praise
Due alone to thy free Grace!
Strength and Merit I disclaim;
Nought is mine but Sin and Shame.

Self-abas'd, O may I feel
My Depravity of Will!
Cause me, more and more, to see
My incessant need of Thee;
Know myself (what well thon know'st)
Viler than the vilest Dust.

Cause me, Lord, to understand;
Take my Heart into thy Hand;
Make me pliant to obey,
Passive as the yielding Clay;
Mightily in me fulfil
All the Pleasure of thy Will.

Of themselves, can lifeless Stones
Rise up into Abraham's Sons?
Can the Æthiop wash him fair?
Figs and Grapes can Thistles bear?

Then might I renew my Heart;
Then may Man himself convert.

Does th' Almighty but persuade?
Suasion cannot raise the Dead:
Nothing, short of Pow'r Divine,
Could subdue a Soul like mine:
Grace omnipotent alone
Could dissolve my Heart of Stone.

First and Last, O Lord, art thou;
Alpha and Omega too:
Thou, who didst thy Grace in-breathe,
Wilt complete the Work of Faith:
Where thou art its Author, there
Thou wilt be its Finisher.

Yes, however Sin oppose,
What Jehovah Wills he Does:
Day by day, his Pow'r I prove;
Sav'd by his constraining Love;
Call'd by his Effectual Word;
Self-destroy'd, and God-restor'd!

FULL ASSURANCE

A debtor to Mercy alone,
Of covenant Mercy I sing;
Nor fear, with thy Righteousness on,
My Person and Off'ring to bring:
The Terrors of Law, and of God,
With me can have nothing to do;
My Saviour's Obedience and Blood
Hide all my Transgressions from view.

The Work, which his Goodness began,
The Arm of his Strength will complete;
His Promise is Yea and Amen,
And never was forfeited yet:
Things future, nor things that are now,
Not all things below nor above,
Can make him his Purpose forego,
Or sever my Soul from his Love.

My Name from the Palms of his Hands
Eternity will not erase;
Impress'd on his Heart it remains
In Marks of indelible Grace:
Yes, I to the End shall endure,
As sure as the Earnest is giv'n;
More happy, but not more secure,
The glorify'd Spirits in Heav'n.

GRACE ACKNOWLEDGED

Form'd for Thyself, and turn'd to Thee,
  Thy Praises, Lord, I shew:
No more, with sacrilegious Pride,
  I rob Thee of thy Due.

Divested of my fancied Plumes,
  I throw me at thy Feet;
Nor, as a Debt, thy Favour claim,
  But, as an Alms, intreat.

Repentance, Holiness, and Faith,
  By which to Thee we live,
Are not Conditions we perform,
  But Graces we receive.

Thy Spirit does not offer Life,
  But raises from the Dead:
And neither asks the Sinner's Leave,
  Nor needs the Sinner's Aid.

Thy Pow'r, before the Fruit is good,
  Must first renew the Tree:
We rise, and work the Works of God,
  When wrought upon by Thee.

Each Grace of our celestial Birth
  From thy blest Influence springs;
Which plants, and nourishes, and guards,
  And to Perfection brings.

Gardens of thine, inclos'd and seal'd,
  Thou all our Works hast wrought;
And wilt eternal Peace ordain
  For those thy Blood hath bought.

Had not thy Love laid hold on us,
  We had not lov'd Thee now:
Possess us quite, thou God of Grace,
  To whom our All we owe!

THE VINE AND THE BRANCHES

JESUS immutably the same,
Thou true and living Vine,
Around thy all-supporting Stem,
My feeble Arms I twine.

Quicken'd by Thee, and kept alive,
I flourish and bear Fruit:
My Life I from thy Sap derive,
My Vigour from thy Root.

Grafted in Thee by Grace alone,
In Growth I daily rise:
And, rais'd on this Foundation-Stone,
My Top shall reach the Skies.

I can do nothing without Thee;
My Strength is wholly thine:
Wither'd and barren should I be,
If sever'd from the Vine.

Upon my Leaf, when parch'd with Heat,
Refreshing Dew shall drop:
The Plant, which thy Right-hand hath set,
Shall ne'er be rooted up.

'Till thou hast led me to the place
Of pure, immortal Joy,
The Riches of thy glorious Grace
Shall all my Need supply.

Who from Eternity decreed
To glorify his own,
Will not forsake the Holy Seed,
Nor take away their Crown.

The Righteous shall hold on their Way,
Nor miss the promis'd Land:
Jesus shall guard them Night and Day,
And hide them in his Hand.

Each Moment water'd by thy Care,
And fenc'd with Pow'r Divine,
Fruit to Eternal Life shall bear
The feeblest Branch of thine.

UNDER DIVINE AWAKENINGS

Thou Fountain of Bliss,
  Thy Smile I intreat;
O'erwhelm'd with Distress,
  I mourn at thy Feet:
The Joy of Salvation,
  When will it be mine?
The high Consolation
  Of Friendship Divine!

Awaken'd to see
  The Depth of my Fall;
For Mercy, on Thee
  I earnestly call:
'Tis thine the lost Sinner
  To save and renew;
Faith's mighty Beginner,
  And Finisher too.

The Light of thy Face
  I wish for alone:
And surely thy Grace
  Hath melted me down;
Else, why do I languish
  Thy Favour to prove?
And wait, with such Anguish,
  A Glimpse of thy Love?

My Righteousness, once
  On which I relied,
Through Grace I renounce,
  In thine to confide:
Thou only wast able
  My Soul to set free,
And shake down my Babel,
  And build me on Thee.

Thy Spirit alone
  Repentance implants,
And gives us to groan
  At feeling our Wants:
'Midst all my Dejection,
  I trust I can raise
Some Marks of Election,
  Some Tokens of Grace.

To Thee I aspire,
  Whose Presence is Heav'n;
Oh, crown the Desire
  Thy Goodness has giv'n:
Nor Satan, nor Nature,
  This Longing could give;
But thou, my Creator,
  By whom I shall live.

Thou wilt not despise
  A Sinner distrest;
All-kind, and all-wise,
  Thy Season is best;
To thy sov'reign Pleasure
  Resign'd would I be;
And tarry thy Leisure,
  And hope still in Thee.

Tho' God may delay
  To show me his Light,
And Heaviness may

Endure for a Night;
Yet Joy in the Morning
Shall surely abound:
No Shadow of turning
With Jesus is found.

That Sinners might claim
The heav'nly Crown,
He went as a Lamb
His Life to lay down:
The Victim was offer'd,
He pour'd out his Blood;
The Guiltless hath suffer'd,
To bring us to God.

Ev'n now he invites
His Mourners to prove
The endless Delights
Which flow from his Love:
To lift us to Heaven
Our Advocate stands;
Our Names are engrav'd on
His Heart and his Hands.

With Sorrow depress,
I groan for Release;
And gladly would taste
How gracious he is:
His Blood fully cleanses;
Ah! when shall I see
He bore *my* Offences,
And suffer'd for *me!*

By Mercy Divine
I'm thus far brought on;
In Weakness, like mine,
Thy Strength is made known:
The Grace thou hast given
(Sure Token for Good)
Shall lead me to Heaven
The City of God.

ANTICIPATION OF GLORY

O it is a sweet Employ
  To bless the God of Love!
This completes the glorious Joy
  Of happier Souls above:
Saints, admitted to the Throne,
  Sing the Grace which brought them there:
Let us, as we journey on,
  The Heav'nly Triumph share.

Yes, we too have cause to sing,
  As we to *Zion* go;
Wonder strikes the grateful String,
  And bids our Bosom glow:
Basking in Thy Smile *they* stand;
  Sinners at Thy Feet *we* fall,
'Till we reach the promis'd Land,
  Where Thou art All in All.

Tho' from Abrah'm's Breast detain'd,
  We travel here awhile;
Thither our Affections tend,
  Where Saints forget their Toil:
With thy Praise upon our Tongues,
  We the Wilderness pass thro';
Trusting soon to mix our Songs
  With their's who see Thee now.

They Thy Promises *fulfill'd,*
  With Shouts of Joy proclaim:
We, to full Redemption *seal'd,*
  And *lov'd alike* with them,
Sing thy never-changing Grace;
  Grace that shall to Glory lead:

Thou, whose Will decreed our Bliss,
 Shalt give the Bliss decreed.

With Thyself and Them on high,
 We humbly trust to shine;
Crown'd with Glory and with Joy
 Inferior but to Thine:
Thee, for our Redemption sold,
 Now exalted to thy Throne,
Eye to Eye we shall behold,
 And know as we are known.

To that high and holy Place
 Where Christ in Person reigns,
Steadfastly we set our Face;
 And He our Strength maintains:
There the ransom'd sing aloud;
 Endless Glory there is found,
Beaming from the Throne of God,
 On all that worship round.

Jesus and his Co-Elect
 One mystic Body make:
All that love him may expect
 His Glory to partake.
When he makes his Jewels up,
 Not a Saint shall wanting be:
O my God, fulfil my Hope,
 And with them reckon *me!*

THANKFULNESS

Why, Lord, art thou so kind to me?
What canst thou in a Sinner see,
  T' excite such Love as thine?
And who am I, that thou shouldst smile,
And crown the vilest of the Vile
  With Blessings so Divine?

No Motive did thy Goodness know,
But that thou *wouldst* Compassion show:
  O sov'reign, matchless Love!
Thy Grace is altogether free;
Else it had never pitch'd on *Me,*
  Nor wrote my Name above.

In me thy farther Pow'r display;
Bid all old things be done away,
  And all things new become:
Me to thy blessed self conform,
And make a poor polluted Worm
  Thy Image and thy Home.

Chose unto Holiness, I long
To bear thy Praises on my Tongue,
  For sanctifying me:
I bless thee for the earnest giv'n;
And wait the Day, when I, in Heav'n,
  Shall quite resemble Thee.

"YE ARE NOT YOUR OWN"

Bought with a Price I am,
And all to Thee belong:
Deign to accept, most gracious Lamb,
The Singer and the Song!

To Thee my Spirit bows,
To Thee my Hopes aspire:
Nail'd to the door-posts of thine house,
I only Thee desire.

Still let my Heart be thine,
Thy Property alone?
No longer would I deem it mine,
Or call myself my own.

Centred in things above
Let my Affections be:
Take all my Heart, thou God of Love,
For all belongs to Thee.

ARMINIANISM RENOUNCED

Giver of ev'ry perfect Gift,
With deep Remorse my Eyes I lift
  To Thee, from whom all good proceeds:
How have I proudly scorn'd to stoop,
And cried the Pow'rs of Nature up,
  And trusted to my legal Deeds!

Blind as I was, nor knew 'twas Thou
Must work in me to will and do;
  Nor felt my Impotence and Sin:
But Jesus claim'd the Soul he bought;
His loving-kindness found me out;
  His Grace compell'd me to come in.

He gave me feelingly to see
My Will was but to Evil free,
  Deprav'd by my first Parent's Fall:
He stirr'd me up to weep and pray,
And made me, in his pow'rful Day,
  Willing to take Him for my All.

Not long the Comforter delay'd;
He brought good tidings to the sad,
  Tidings of everlasting Peace:
And now rejoicing I go on,
'Till summon'd to receive the Crown
  Due to my Saviour's Righteousness.

CHRIST'S INTERCESSION

Awake, sweet Gratitude, and sing
    Th' ascended Saviour's Love;
Tell how he lives to carry on
    His People's Cause above.

Not as a Supplicant he stands,
    But challenges his own:
Seated he prays: a regal Priest!
    A Priest upon his Throne.

With Cries and Tears he offer'd up
    His humble Suit below;
But with Authority he asks,
    Enthron'd in Glory now.

For all, that come to God by Him,
    Salvation he demands;
Points to their Names upon his Breast,
    And spreads his wounded Hands.

His Covenant and Sacrifice
    Give Sanction to his Claim:
"Father, I will that all my Saints
    Be with me where I am:

"By their Salvation, recompense
    The Sorrows I endur'd;
Just to the Merits of thy Son,
    And faithful to thy Word."

Founded on Right, his Pray'r avails:
    The Father never can
From his Anointed turn away,
    Nor hear him ask in vain.

Eternal Life, at his Request,
To ev'ry Saint is giv'n:
Safety on Earth, and, after Death,
The Plenitude of Heav'n.

Lord, I believe Thou didst go up,
To plead our Cause with God:
And now thou in thy Kingdom art,
Remember Me for good!

Let the much Incense of thy Pray'r
In my Behalf ascend;
And as its Virtue, so my Praise,
Shall never, never end.

THE METHOD OF SALVATION

Thee, Father, we bless,
Whose distinguishing Grace
Selected a People to show forth thy praise.

Nor is thy Love known
By Election alone;
For, O! thou hast added the Gift of thy Son.

The goodness in vain
We attempt to explain,
Which found and accepted a Ransom for Men.

Great Surety of Thine,
Thou didst not decline
To concur with the Father's most gracious design:

In his Book of Decree,
It was written of Thee,
That thou shouldst accomplish Salvation for me.

Thou stood'st in our stead,
As our Covenant-Head,
E'er Sin had a Footing, or Adam was made.

With Joy we've beheld
Our Sentence repeal'd:
And sing thy Eternal Engagements fulfill'd.

To Jesus our Friend
Our Thanks shall ascend,
Who saves to the utmost, and loves to the end.

Our Ransom he paid;
In his Merit array'd,
We attain to the Glory for which we were made.

Sweet Spirit of Grace,
Thy Mercy we bless
For Thy eminent Share in the Council of Peace.

Great Agent Divine,
To restore us is thine,
And cause us afresh in thy Likeness to shine.

O God, 'tis thy Part
To convince and convert;
To give a new Life, and create a new Heart.

By thy Presence and Grace
We're upheld in our Race,
And are kept in thy Love to the End of our days.

Father, Spirit, and Son
Agree thus in one,
The Salvation of those He has mark'd for his own.

Let Us, too, agree
To glorify Thee,
Thou ineffable One, thou adorable Three!

"WHOM HAVE I IN HEAVEN"

Whom have I in Heav'n but Thee
 That can thy Creature bless?
What were all the Earth to me,
 If Stranger to thy Peace?
All is Vanity but Christ;
 Pain, and Darkness, and Despair,
Rankle in a Sinner's Breast,
 Till thou art present there.

If my Lord his Love reveal,
 No other Bliss I want;
He my ev'ry Wound can Heal,
 And silence each Complaint:
He, that suffer'd in my Stead,
 Must the great Physician be;
I cannot be comforted,
 'Till comforted by Thee.

Thee, thou know'st, I wish to love,
 For which thy Name I bless;
Pour thy Spirit from above,
 Upon my waiting Fleece!
Gentle as descending Dew,
 Welcome as reviving Show'rs,
Let him my Election shew,
 And gild my gloomy Hours.

Yet, if so thou seest fit,
 'Tis best for me to mourn:
Still my Hold I cannot quit,
 Nor from my Refuge turn.

This, by Grace, my Song shall be,
  As I to thy Kingdom go:
Whom have I in Heav'n but Thee?
And whom, but Thee, below?

FAITH FAINTING

Encompass'd with Clouds of Distress,
Just ready all Hope to resign,
I pant for the Light of thy Face,
And fear it will never be mine:
Dishearten'd with waiting so long,
I sink at thy Feet with my Load;
All-plaintive I pour out my Song,
And stretch forth my Hands unto God.

Shine, Lord, and my Terror shall cease;
The Blood of Atonement apply;
And lead me to Jesus for Peace,
The Rock that is higher than I:
Speak, Saviour, for sweet is thy Voice;
Thy Presence is fair to behold:
I thirst for thy Spirit with Cries
And Groanings that cannot be told.

If sometimes I strive, as I mourn,
My Hold of thy Promise to keep,
The Billows more fiercely return,
And plunge me again in the Deep:
While harrass'd, and cast from thy Sight,
The Tempter suggests, with a Roar,
"The Lord hath forsaken thee quite:
Thy God will be gracious no more."

Yet, Lord, if thy Love hath design'd
No Covenant-Blessing for me,
Ah tell me, How is it I find
Some sweetness in waiting for Thee?

Almighty to rescue Thou art;
  Thy Grace is my only Resource:
If e'er Thou art Lord of my Heart,
  Thy Spirit must take it by Force.

FAITH REVIVING

From whence this Fear and Unbelief?
Hath not the Father put to Grief
His spotless Son for me?
And will the righteous Judge of Men,
Condemn me for that Debt of Sin,
Which, Lord, was charg'd on Thee?

Complete Atonement Thou hast made,
And to the utmost Farthing paid
Whate'er thy People ow'd:
Nor can his Wrath on me take place,
If shelter'd in thy Righteousness,
And sprinkled with thy Blood.

If Thou hast my Discharge procur'd,
And freely in my Room endur'd
The whole of Wrath Divine:
Payment GOD cannot *twice* demand,
First at my bleeding Surety's hand,
And then again at mine.

If Thou for me hast purchas'd Faith
By thy Obedience unto Death,
He will the Grace bestow:
Would Israel's God a Price receive,
And not the purchas'd blessing give?
His Justice answers, No!

Turn then, my Soul, unto thy Rest;
The Merits of thy great High Priest
Have bought thy Liberty:
Trust in his efficacious Blood;
Nor fear thy Banishment from God,
Since Jesus died for Thee.

WEAK BELIEVERS ENCOURAGED

Your Harps, ye trembling Saints,
Down from the Willows take:
Loud to the Praise of Love Divine,
Bid ev'ry String awake.
Tho' in a foreign Land,
We are not far from Home:
And nearer to our House above
We ev'ry Moment come.

His Grace will to the End
Stronger and brighter shine;
Nor present Things, nor Things to come,
Shall quench the Spark Divine.
Fasten'd within the Vail,
Hope be your Anchor strong;
His loving Spirit, the sweet Gale
That wafts you smooth along.

Or, should the Surges rise,
And Peace delay to come;
Blest is the Sorrow, kind the Storm,
That drives us nearer Home.
The People of his Choice
He will not cast away;
Yet do not always here expect
On Tabor's Mount to stay.

When we in Darkness walk,
Nor feel the heav'nly Flame;
Then is the Time to trust our God,
And rest upon his Name.
Soon shall our Doubts and Fears
Subside at his Control:

His Loving-kindness shall break through
The Midnight of the Soul.

No Wonder, when his Love
Pervades your kindling Breast,
You wish for ever to retain
The heart-transporting Guest.
Yet learn, in ev'ry State,
To make his Will your own;
And when the Joys of Sense depart,
To walk by Faith alone.

By anxious Fear depress'd,
When, from the Deep, ye mourn,
"Lord, why so hasty to depart,
So tedious in return?"
Still on his plighted Love,
At all events rely:
The very Hidings of his Face
Shall train thee up to Joy.

Wait, 'till the Shadows flee;
Wait, thy appointed Hour:
Wait, 'till the Bridegroom of thy Soul
Reveals his Love with Pow'r.
The Time of Love will come,
When thou shalt clearly see,
Not only that he shed his Blood,
But that it flowed for Thee!

Tarry his Leisure then,
Altho' he seem to stay:
A Moment's Intercourse with him,
Thy Grief will over-pay.

Blest is the man, O God,
That stays himself on Thee!
Who wait for thy Salvation, Lord,
Shall thy Salvation see.

CHRIST ALL IN ALL

Compar'd with Christ, in all beside
  No Comeliness I see;
The one Thing needful, dearest Lord,
  Is to be one with Thee.
The Sense of thy expiring Love
  Into my Soul convey:
Thyself Bestow; for Thee alone
  I absolutely pray.

Whatever else thy Will withholds,
  Here grant me to succeed:
O let Thyself my Portion be,
  And I am blest indeed.
Less than Thyself will not suffice,
  My Comfort to restore:
More than Thyself I cannot have;
  And Thou canst give no more.

Lov'd of my God, for Him again
  With Love intense I burn:
Chosen of Thee e'er Time began,
  I choose Thee in return.
Whate'er consists not with thy Love,
  O teach me to resign:
I'm rich to all th' Intents of Bliss,
  If Thou, O God, art mine.

HAPPINESS FOUND

Happiness, thou lovely Name,
  Where's thy Seat, O tell me, where?
Learning, Pleasure, Wealth, and Fame,
  All cry out, "It is not here":
Not the Wisdom of the Wise
Can inform me where it lies,
Not the Grandeur of the Great
Can the Bliss I seek create.

Object of my first Desire,
  JESUS, crucified for me!
All to Happiness aspire,
  Only to be found in thee:
Thee to please, and thee to know,
Constitute our Bliss below;
Thee to see and thee to love,
Constitute our Bliss above.

Lord, it is not Life to live,
  If thy Presence thou deny:
Lord, if thou thy Presence give,
  'Tis no longer Death to die:
Source and Giver of Repose,
Singly from thy Smile it flows;
Peace and Happiness are thine;
Mine they are, if Thou art mine.

Whilst I feel thy Love to me,
  Ev'ry object teems with Joy,
Here, O may I walk with Thee,
  Then into thy Presence Die!

Let me but Thyself possess,
Total Sum of Happiness!
Real Bliss I then shall prove;
Heav'n below, and Heav'n above.

TO THE TRINITY

Eternal Hallelujahs
Be to the FATHER giv'n,
    Who lov'd his own
    Ere Time begun,
And mark'd them out for Heav'n.

Anthems of equal Glory
Ascribe we to the SAVIOUR;
    Who liv'd and died,
    That we, his Bride,
Might live with him for ever.

Hail, co-eternal SPIRIT,
Thy Church's new Creator!
    The Saints he seals,
    Their Fear dispels,
And sanctifies their Nature.

We Laud the glorious TRIAD,
The mystic One in essence;
    Till call'd to join
    The Hosts that shine,
In his immediate Presence.

Faithful is He that promis'd,
And stands engag'd to save us:
    The Tri-une Lord
    Has pass'd his Word
That He will never leave us.

A Kingdom he assign'd us,
Before the World's foundation:
    Thou God of Grace,
    Be thine the Praise,
And ours the Consolation.

HOW VAST THE BENEFITS DIVINE

Who hath saved us.—2 TIMOTHY 1:9.

How vast the Benefits divine,
Which we in Christ possess!
Sav'd from the Guilt of Sin we are,
And call'd to Holiness.

But not for Works which we have done,
Or shall hereafter do,
Hath God decreed on sinful Worms
Salvation to bestow.

The Glory, Lord, from first to last,
Is due to Thee alone:
Aught to ourselves we dare not take,
Or rob Thee of thy Crown.

Our glorious Surety undertook
To satisfy for Man,
And Grace was given us, in Him,
Before the World began.

This is thy Will, that in thy Love
We ever should abide:
And lo; we Earth and Hell defy,
To make thy Counsel void.

Not one of all the chosen Race,
But shall to Heav'n attain;
Partake, on Earth, the purpos'd Grace,
And then with JESUS reign.

Of Father, Son, and Spirit, we
Extol the threefold Care;
Whose Love, whose Merit, and whose Pow'r
Unite to lift us there.

A CHAMBER HYMN

What tho' my frail Eyelids refuse
Continual watching to keep,
And, punctual, as Midnight renews,
Demand the refreshment of Sleep;
A sov'reign Protector I have,
Unseen, yet for ever at hand:
Unchangeably faithful to save,
Almighty to rule and command.

From Evil secure, and its dread,
I rest, if my Saviour is nigh;
And Songs his kind presence indeed
Shall in the Night-season supply:
He smiles, and my Comforts abound;
His grace as the Dew shall descend,
And Walls of Salvation surround
The Soul He delights to defend.

Kind Author and Ground of my Hope,
Thee, Thee for my God I avow;
My glad Ebenezer set up,
And own Thou hast help'd me till now:
I muse on the Years that are past,
Wherein my Defence thou hast prov'd;
Nor wilt thou relinquish, at last,
A Sinner so signally lov'd.

Beneficent Hearer of Pray'r,
Thou Feeder and Guardian of thine,
My All to thy covenant Care
I, sleeping and waking, resign:
If thou art my Shield and my Sun,
The Night is no darkness to me;

And, fast as my Moments roll on,
They bring me but nearer to Thee.

Thy minist'ring Spirits descend,
And watch while thy Saints are asleep;
By Day and by Night they attend,
The Heirs of Salvation to keep:
Bright Seraphs, dispatch'd from the Throne,
Fly swift to their Stations assign'd;
And Angels elect are sent down
To guard the elect of Mankind.

Thy Worship no interval knows:
Their Fervour is still on the Wing;
And, while they protect my Repose,
They Chant to the praise of my King:
I, too, at the Season ordain'd,
Their Chorus for ever shall join;
And Love and Adore, without end,
Their gracious Creator and mine.

A LIVING AND DYING PRAYER FOR THE HOLIEST BELIEVER IN THE WORLD

Rock of Ages, cleft for me,
Let me hide myself in Thee!
Let the Water and the Blood,
From thy riven Side which flow'd,
Be of Sin the double Cure,
Cleanse me from its Guilt and Pow'r.

Not the Labours of my Hands
Can fulfil thy Law's demands:
Could my Zeal no respite know,
Could my Tears for ever flow,
All for Sin could not atone:
Thou must save, and Thou alone!

Nothing in my Hand I bring;
Simply to thy Cross I cling;
Naked, come to Thee for Dress;
Helpless, look to Thee for Grace;
Foul, I to the Fountain fly:
Wash me, SAVIOUR, or I die!

Whilst I draw this fleeting Breath—
When my Eye-strings break in Death—
When I soar through tracts unknown—
See Thee on thy Judgment-Throne—
ROCK of Ages, cleft for me,
Let me hide myself in THEE!

"MY MEDITATION OF HIM SHALL BE SWEET"

My meditation of him shall be sweet: I will be glad in the Lord.
—Psalm 104:34.

(Written in Illness.)

When Langour and Disease invade
This trembling House of Clay;
'Tis sweet to look beyond the Cage,
And long to fly away.

Sweet to look inward and attend
The Whispers of his Love;
Sweet to look upward to the place
Where Jesus pleads above.

Sweet to look back and see my Name
In Life's fair Book set down;
Sweet to look forward and behold
Eternal Joys my own.

Sweet to reflect how Grace divine
My Sins on Jesus laid;
Sweet to remember that his Blood
My debt of sufferings paid.

Sweet on his Righteousness to stand,
Which saves from second Death;
Sweet to experience Day by Day,
His Spirit's quick'ning Breath.

Sweet on his Faithfulness to rest,
Whose Love can never end:
Sweet on his Covenant of Grace,
For all Things to depend.

Sweet in the confidence of Faith,
To trust his firm Decrees;
Sweet to lie passive in his Hand,
And know no Will but his.

Sweet to rejoice in lively Hope,
That, when my Change shall come,
Angels will hover round my Bed,
And waft my Spirit Home.

There shall my disimprison'd Soul
Behold Him and adore;
Be with his Likeness satisfied,
And grieve and sin no more.

Shall see him wear that very Flesh
On which my Guilt was lain;
His Love intense, his Merit fresh,
As tho' but newly slain.

Soon, too, my slumb'ring Dust shall hear
The Trumpet's quick'ning sound;
And, by my Saviour's power rebuilt,
At his right Hand be found.

These Eyes shall see him in that Day,
The God that died for me;
And all my rising Bones shall say,
Lord, who is like to Thee?

If such the Views which grace unfolds,
Weak as it is below,
What raptures must the Church above
In Jesu's presence know!

If such the sweetness of the Stream,
  What must the Fountain be,
Where Saints and Angels draw their Bliss
  Immediately from thee?

O may the Unction of these Truths,
  For ever with me stay;
'Till from her sinful Cage dismiss'd
  My Spirit flies away.

THE DYING BELIEVER TO HIS SOUL

Deathless principle arise;
Soar thou native of the Skies,
Pearl of price by JESUS bought,
To his glorious Likeness wrought,
Go to shine before his Throne;
Deck his Mediatorial Crown;
Go, his triumphs to adorn;
Made for God, to God return.

Lo, he beckons from on High!
Fearless to his presence fly:
Thine the merit of his Blood;
Thine the righteousness of God.
Angels, joyful to attend,
Hov'ring, round thy Pillow bend;
Wait to catch the Signal giv'n,
And escort thee quick to Heav'n.

Is thy earthly House distrest?
Willing to retain her Guest?
'Tis not thou, but she, must die;
Fly, celestial Tenant, fly.
Burst thy Shackles, drop thy Clay,
Sweetly breathe thyself away,
Singing, to thy Crown remove;
Swift of Wing, and fir'd with Love.

Shudder not to pass the Stream;
Venture all thy Care on him;
Him, whose dying Love and Pow'r
Still'd its tossing, hush'd its Roar.
Safe is th' expanded Wave;
Gentle as a Summer's eve;

Not one Object of his Care
Ever suffer'd shipwreck there.

See the Haven full in view;
Love divine shall bear thee through!
Trust to that propitious Gale;
Weigh thy Anchor, spread thy Sail.
Saints in Glory perfect made,
Wait thy Passage through the Shade;
Ardent for thy coming o'er,
See, they throng the blissful Shore.

Mount, their Transports to improve:
Join the longing Choir above;
Swiftly to their Wish be given:
Kindle higher Joy in Heaven.
Such the Prospects that arise
To the dying Christian's Eyes;
Such the glorious Vista Faith
Opens through the Shades of Death!

LEANING ON THE BELOVED

Courage, my Soul, Jehovah speaks,
 His Promise is for thee:
"I never will forsake nor leave
 The Soul betroth'd to me."

The cheering Word, as Heav'nly Dew.
 My thirsty Soul drinks in:
JESUS commands me to Rejoice,
 Who bore away my Sin.

My Saviour's ever-watchful Eye,
 Is over me for Good:
What will he not on me bestow
 Who hath himself bestow'd?

Me to enrich, himself he made
 Poor, and of no esteem:
The Source, the true Foundation, this
 Of all my Love to him.

Dear Lord, into thy faithful Hands,
 My welfare I commit;
And to thy Righteousness alone,
 For safety I retreat.

Sorrows and Agonies and Death,
 Thou didst endure for me.
When all the Sins of God's Elect
 Were made to meet on thee.

Tho' worthy, in myself, of Hell,
 And everlasting Shame;
I cannot dread the Frown divine,
 Accepted in the Lamb.

Still on thy Merit, gracious Lord,
  Enable me to lean:
Ever in Thee may I be found,
  My hiding-place from Sin!

Exult, my Soul; thy safety stands
  Unshaken as his Throne;
His People's everlasting Life
  Is founded on his own.

WE HAVE BOLDNESS TO ENTER INTO THE HOLIEST BY THE BLOOD OF JESUS

(Hebrews 10:19)

O Precious Blood, O glorious Death,
By which the Sinner Lives!
When stung with Sin, this Blood we view,
And all our Joy revives.

We flourish as the water'd Herb,
Who keep this Blood in sight,
The Blood that chases our Distress,
And makes our Garments White.

The Blood that purchas'd our release,
And washes out our Stains,
We challenge Earth and Hell to show
A Sin it cannot cleanse.

Our scarlet Crimes are made as Wool,
And we brought nigh to God;
Thanks to that Wrath-appeasing Death;
That Heav'n-procuring Blood.

The Blood that makes his glorious Church
From ev'ry Blemish Free;
And, O, the riches of his Love!
He pour'd it out for me.

Guilty and worthless as I am,
It all for me was giv'n;
And boldness, through his Blood, I have
To enter into Heav'n.

Thither, in my great Surety's right,
I surely shall be brought!

He could not Agonize in vain,
Nor spend his Strength for nought.

He wills that I, and all his Sheep,
Should reign with him in Bliss;
And Pow'r he has to execute
Whate'er his Will decrees.

The Father's everlasting Love,
And Jesus' precious blood,
Shall be our endless Themes of Praise,
In yonder blest Abode.

In Patience let us then possess
Our Souls 'till He appear:
Our Head already is in Heav'n,
And we shall soon be there.

TO THE BLESSED SPIRIT[1]

Holy Ghost, dispel our Sadness,
   Pierce the Clouds of sinful Night:
Come, thou source of sweetest Gladness,
   Breathe thy Life, and spread thy Light!
Loving Spirit, God of Peace,
Great distributer of Grace,
   Rest upon this Congregation!
   Hear, O hear our Supplication.

From that Height which knows no Measure,
   As a gracious Show'r descend;
Bringing down the richest Treasure
   Man can wish, and God can send:
O thou Glory, shining down
From the Father and the Son,
   Grant us thy Illumination!
   Rest upon this Congregation.

Come, thou best of all Donations
   God can give, or we implore;
Having thy sweet Consolations,
   We need wish for nothing more.
Come, with Unction, and with Pow'r;
On our Souls thy Graces show'r;
   Author of the New Creation,
   Make our Hearts thy Habitation.

Known to Thee are all recesses
   Of the Earth and spreading Skies;
Every Sand the Shore possesses,

---

1 Altered from "O thou sweetest Source of Gladness," by J. C. Jacobi, 1725. Original by Paul Gerhardt.

Thy omniscient Mind descries:
Holy Fountain, wash us clean,
Both from Error, and from Sin;
Make us fly what Thou refusest,
And delight in what Thou choosest.

Manifest thy Love for ever;
Fence us in on every Side;
In Distress be our Reliever;
Guard, and teach, support, and guide:
Let thy kind, effectual Grace
Turn our Feet from evil Ways:
Shew thyself our New Creator,
And conform us to thy Nature.

Be our Friend on each Occasion,
God, omnipotent to save!
When we die, be our Salvation;
When we're buried, be our Grave:
And, when from the Grave we rise,
Take us up above the Skies;
Seat us with thy Saints in Glory,
There for ever to adore Thee.

FIRST LINE INDEX

AUTHORSHIP OF HYMNS

Mr. Walter Row, the editor of the works of Toplady, and other compilers of Hymn books, having attributed several hymns to Toplady which are not his, the publisher of this volume has drawn up the following correct list of the real authors, with the sources from which those hymns have been taken.

Astonish'd and distress'd—B. Beddome's Hymns, Hymn 469
Blow ye the Trumpet, blow—C. Wesley, Hymns for N.Y.D., 1751, p. 6
Christ, whose Glory fills the Skies—C. Wesley, H. & S. P. 1740, p. 24
Come, guilty Souls, and flee away—J. Humphrey—Cennick's Hymns, p. 87
Come Holy Ghost, our Souls inspire—Anc. Hymn, M. H. B., 1754, pt. 1, p. 130
Father, I want a thankful Heart—C. Wesley, H. & S. P., 1743, pp. 54–64
Hail! God the Father! at whose Call—S. Wesley's Poems, 1743, p. 319
Hail! God the Son! to Glory crown'd—S. Wesley's Poems, 1743, p. 320
Hail! Holy Ghost! Jehovah! Third—S. Wesley's Poems, 1743, p. 321
Hail! Holy, Holy, Holy, Lord!—S. Wesley's Poems, 1743, p. 322
Hail, mighty Jesus! how divine—B. Wallin's Hymns, 1750, p. 95
I groan from Sin to be set free—C. Wesley, H. & S. P., 1740, p. 20
Jesus, at thy Command—R. De Courcy. Collection, 1793, p. 217
Jesus, Lover of my Soul—C. Wesley, H. & S. P., 1740, p. 57
Jesus, what hast thou bestow'd?—C. Wesley, H. & S. P., 1742, p. 206
Let the World their Virtue boast—C. Wesley, H. & S. P., 1742, p. 259
Light of those whose dreary Dwelling—C. Wesley, Nativity Hymns, 1751, p. 15
Love divine, all Loves excelling—C. Wesley, Redemption Hymns, p. 13
O when shall we, supremely blest—C. Wesley, Intercession Hymns, p. 29
Prepare me, gracious God!—R. Elliot's Hymns, 1761, p. 126
Rejoice, ye Saints, in ev'ry State—B. Wallin's Hymns, 1750, p. 29
Source of Light, and Pow'r divine—W. Shirley, L. H. Coll., Hymn 136
The Pow'r of Hell, the Strength of Sin—C. Wesley, H. & S. P., 1742, p. 181
Thou Shepherd of Israel divine—C. Wesley, S. S. H., 1762, vol. 1, p. 294
Thrice comfortable Hope—C. Wesley, H. & S. P., 1749, vol. 2, p. 305
Thy Anger for what I have done—C. Wesley, S. S. H., 1762, vol. 2, p. 93
'Tis finish'd!—The *Messiah* dies—C. Wesley, S. S. H., 1762, vol. 2, p. 234

'Tis pleasant to sing—C. Wesley, S. S. H., 1762, vol. 1, p. 283
What in thy Love possess I not?—P. Gerhardt, H. & S. P., 1743, p. 103
What tho' I cannot break my chain—C. Wesley, H. & S. P., 1740, p. 80

ABBREVIATIONS:—N. Y. D., *New Year's Day;* H. & S. P., *Hymns and Sacred Poems;* M. H. B., *Moravian Hymn Book;* L. H. Coll., *Lady Huntingdon's Collection;* S. S. H., *Short Scripture Hymns.*

Made in the USA
Middletown, DE
25 June 2018